Traveling Through
ROUGH WATERS

JAMES R. PRYCE, M.DIV.

Limited First Edition

Copyright © 2013 by JAMES R. PRYCE

All rights reserved. Printed in the United States of America.

Library of Congress cataloging number:

PRYCE, JAMES R. / Travelling through rough waters

ISBN # 978-0-9892644-9-5

The author assumes full responsibility for the accuracy of all facts and quotations cited in this manuscript. No part of this work may be reproduced or transmitted in any form electronic or mechanical, including photocopying, recording, or by any retrieval system without written permission from the publisher/author.

Published by: New Cyber Ministry Inc.

Please reach the author at his website: www.newcyberministry.com.

Contents

Introduction	1
Chapter 1: Running to win	4
Chapter 2: Strength for the Journey	13
Chapter 3: Touched by an Angel	26
Chapter 4: What in Hell Do You Want?	37
Chapter 5: The Seven Last Plagues	49
Chapter 6: Traveling on Rough Waters	69
Chapter 7: The Great Gulf Fixed	92
Chapter 8: The People of the Kingdom	99
Chapter 9: Ye That Dwelleth in God shall Find Hope	108
Chapter 10: The Mark of the Beast	118
Chapter 11: The Armor of God	138
Chapter 12: Dead Man Walking	151
Chapter 13: City in Space	163
Chapter 14: The Father – The Son – The Holy Spirit	174
Chapter 15: Before the evil days come	189
Chapter 16: Who Changed It?	202
Chapter 17: The Test	215
Chapter 18: Breaking free from the stronghold of my past	227
Chapter 19: The Unwanted List	239
Chapter 20: If My People Would Pray	259
Chapter 21: How Does One Get to Be in God's Hall of Fame?	271
Chapter 22: Homosexuals - and the Bible	286

Introduction

To win a race requires more than just having the ability to run. The runner must know the rules of the game, he must study his opponent, he must have his physical checkup to make sure that he or she is physically fit, and he must understand the psychology of running. If you go to the racetrack, you would notice that those horses are well prepared. The trainers take out the horses for exercise to keep their skills and bodies in maximum shape. The vets come and make their regular medical checkups to make sure the horses are in good health. Traveling on rough waters is similar in many ways to running a race. Both ideas have to do with the reality of the Christian

Travelling Through Rough Waters

life. The captain should know the dynamic and movements of the water. He must also understand the dynamic and movements of the wind. There are times he has to drop sail and let the ship be carried by the wind.

As our spiritual ship sets sail, how do we manage the rolling billows and wind that seek to damage and overturn our ship, or if our spiritual life takes the position of a runner, how do we prepare to run the race of life? How do we run to win? There are many things that can hinder us from winning or reaching our destination. This book is designed to look at some of those obstacles that can hinder us from winning as we run the race of life, or reaching our destination as we set sail on our spiritual ship.

I heard a story about an African runner who was known to be one of the world's best athletes. Many of his opponents studied his profile to see how they could defeat him, but no one could unlock the secret of his ability to defeat those who ran in a race with him. After many years of trying to understand the psychology of this young man, an individual came up with an idea; he decided to strategically place individuals in the bushes along the pathway with little red balls and as the runner was passing by, they would throw their little red balls in front of the runner.

Unconsciously the runner would slow down to see this little red ball. Finally, he was distracted enough and was overtaken by his opponent and lost the race. Satan is a master psychologist and he studies the people of God who are running the spiritual race for life, and he has little red balls of distraction, and he uses people from all

Introduction

walks of life to throw his little red balls. Sometimes he uses a family member, sometimes a friend, sometimes professionals, sometimes politicians, and sometimes he uses religious leaders to throw out his little red balls of distraction.

My aim in this book is to alert my readers to some of the pitfalls and distractions that Satan is using to confuse, distract, and destroy God's people who are running the race of life. I coined for myself the name, "The Biblical Reporter"; therefore, I search the scripture and when I find precious gems I report them to my readers. So as you read this book, remember that I am just the reporter. I am reporting what I found as I look for distraction on the runner's path, or on the high windy seas and the rolling billows as the children of God set sail on their spiritual ship.

Chapter 1

Running to win

The road to life everlasting is filled with obstacles, and Christians must understand this reality and prepare to deal with it. There are some people who believe that Christians are weaklings, but this idea is far away from the truth. A child of God is one of the strongest persons on planet earth, spiritually and morally. Being able to tell somebody off or curse someone when they have done something wrong to you or make you upset is very easy, anybody can curse somebody.

Running to win

When someone does wrong things to you and abuses you, whether physically or psychologically, and you are able to hold your peace, you can safely say that you are becoming a mature man or a mature woman. A strong man or woman has the ability not to speak when they could have spoken and return a soft answer when an angry blow is thrown at them.

Paul was writing to the Philippian believers, and as he was about to close the letter, he said, "Finally my brethren, beware of evil men and women in the church who believe that everyone has to be like them to be saved. Some of you are so zealous of the cause of God and want to defend its purity at the expense of hurting others, but if anyone should be zealous it should me. I was born of the Tribe of Benjamin, circumcised on the eight day, highly trained in the Law at the school of Gemellia. Speaking of zeal, I persecuted the churches from Don to Beersheba. But now, I count all of those things as rubbish. To gain Christ means more to me than of those previous things I used to be so zealous about.

Brethren, I do not consider myself to have laid hold [that is, on the prize from heaven], but one thing I do: Forget the things which lie behind me and I stretch toward the gold that lies before me. I press forward and I hasten to run after the prize of the upward calling in Christ Jesus." (Phil. 3:1-14)

Now, verses 13 and 14 are loaded. I would not do justice to this subject if I pass by without saying a single word of how loaded these verses are. In verse 13 Paul said he is forgetting the things of the past; but there's one important thing here: Paul wrote the word in the

Travelling Through Rough Waters

present middle participle; therefore, if you must translate the word in its rightful form, you should say, "I am continually making myself forget the past, or I am intentionally putting out of my mind the things of the past." Now, Paul just laid down the premise of the Christian's survival as he or she runs the race of life. Christians cannot run around with baggage and expect to make it. Your load is too heavy to carry. You got to block out the hateful feelings. You must block out the desire to be Number One in everything you do. You must block out the desire to hurt people who you may not like. You will have to block out the desire to act as if you are better than everybody else. You will have to block out the lackadaisical feelings when it comes to your religion. You will have to block out the thoughts that your husband or your wife is no good, and that you are going to tell him or her a few things.

You will have to block out the idea that makes you think that you can enjoy the world and go to heaven at the same time. You've got to block out the desire to curse people when you get mad at them. This is not a normal forgetfulness due to one's inability to remember things. Paul is telling us to deliberately block things out of our minds so that our load will be lighter as we run the race of life. Paul made himself forget that he was born of the Tribe of Benjamin. (In biblical days and even in some Jewish families today, family heritage means a lot to a Jewish man.) But sometimes who we are becomes a barrier in running the race successfully. We look in the church to see if there is anybody like us so we can associate with him or her, because I do not want to mingle with a certain class of people in the church.

Paul made himself forget that he was trained at the school of Gemellia. Sometime our education can get in our way. Someone may graduate from Harvard University and he or she may thinks that there is no one in the church who is up to his caliber. He may say in his mind, "I do not see anyone in the church to converse with." so during Bible class he just sits there with his dignified self, too educated to speak. Paul made himself forget that he had a thorn in his flesh. Sometime we get upset with the Lord because our thorn is still there, but anything Paul recognized that could be an obstacle or a barrier as he ran the race for life, he blocked it out of his mind.

In verse 14 he said, I am pressing or scratching to the mark. Again he spoke in the present middle participle, and so it should be interpreted as: "I am making myself press, or I am making myself stretch to the mark." I deliberately block out of mind everything that I may contemplate on stretching toward the mark of the higher calling. So when you slip sometimes as we always do, and somebody is ready to talk about you, tell him you are stretching toward the mark of the higher calling. When your friends and loved ones notice that your behavior has changed for the better, and they are concerned, thinking that something is wrong because you used to behave differently, tell them you are stretching toward the mark of the higher calling. When you have grown weary about the journey before you, and you feel like turning around, you must ignore your pain and tell yourself I am stretching and I am pressing toward the mark

Travelling Through Rough Waters

of the higher calling.

Paul used the runner as a contrast for the Christian who is heading home toward heaven. As he sets his spiritual eyes towards heaven, he should not allow anything to get in his way or distract him. His eyes must be fixed on Jesus who is the mark and the prize. As the runner heads home, his eyes must be fixed. His mind must be set. His body must be bent forward toward heaven, and his hands and feet must be bent and stretching toward the prize before him. It is sad to say, but there are some people who run the race of life as though they have nothing to lose. Their interest seems to be very shallow; they are tossed about by every impulse and every wind of circumstance.

But we must learn to run for our lives because our ungodly nature will make a steel on us. It will exert a paralyzing influence on our mind. You don't believe it, and linger around forbidding areas and see what happens. First of all, you will find yourself debating and rationalizing about something you know that you should not do. The thought lingers on in your mind and you try to find reasons why it is okay to do. Some of us get into what they call psychological dissonance (that means certain basic principles are being interfered with, or you could say there is a quarrel that has broken out in your mind). If we do not make ourselves forget those thoughts, we will find ourselves doing the very thing we told ourselves that we would not do. You know what happens when we find ourselves doing what we said we would not do? Our falling nature or our desire paralyzes our will and takes over. In the human race, only one individual wins at a given time, but the race for heaven is different; everyone who continues to run will win because the race is not for the swift or the slow but for the one who continues to run. Some Christians run the race of life very carelessly because they have very little to lose.

There is a story about a pack of dogs that were chasing a rabbit. One of the dog said to the other dogs, "Drop out of the chase and let me show you how to chase a rabbit." The rest of dogs stop chasing the rabbit leaving only one dog who claimed that he knew how to catch a rabbit. The rabbit was much faster than the dog and he made a quick get-a way. After a while the dog came back limping and the rest of dogs asked him, what happen? Where is the rabbit? The limping dog responded, "He was running for his life, but I was just running for the fun of chasing rabbit." Christians must understand that we have much to lose, therefore, we must run for our very life. We must run and never look back because our very lives depend on our speed and swiftness. We must make ourselves Press and Stretch. Do not let the things of this world hold you back. We must press on because this is the only way to inherit eternal life. Some people want to wear the crown, but they do not want to carry the cross. Some people talk religion by the mile, but they live it by the inch. Some people want to go to heaven while enjoying the things of this world, but you and I can't have both worlds. Pressing on implies hard work. Salvation is free, but the process of sanctification is not. The mind must be disciplined by the Word of God. The appetite must be controlled. The tongue must be tamed.

Talking about one another must be stopped. Living

Travelling Through Rough Waters

together in brotherly cohesiveness must be encouraged. We must understand that the idea of pressing on is not an easy process. One moment we are up on a spiritual mountaintop, the next moment it seems as if we are down in the valley of dry bone, cut off from the spring of living water that flowed in our souls yesterday. We must come to the conclusion that even when it seems as if our world is turning upside down, we must press on. We must press on even when it seems as if we are not moving. Sometimes it seems as if some sin will not go away. We fast about them. We pray about them. We make a conscientious effort over and over, but they will not go away. Don't give up, make yourself press on, make yourself forget the many times that you have failed and press on.

As we press on we need to take Jesus with us, because He is the light that shines in darkness. The world is getting darker than a thousand midnights. Friends and loved ones will talk about you behind your back and turn away from you. You must get to the place where you learn to press on alone with Jesus, because the armies of flesh will fail you, you dare not trust your own. Joshua had gotten to a place in his life where he learned to press on alone with Jesus. After watching God's activity for forty years in the wilderness and the Israelites' triumphant victory in Canaan, he looked at the church and saw their inconsistencies, he made his final appeal to them, he said as for me and my house we will press on alone with Jesus. Shadrach, Meshach and Abednego knew how to press on alone. Down there in Babylon, the king brought everybody before him and commanded the people to cast themselves down before the golden image. The music began to play and everybody bowed down, everybody except Shadrach, Meshach, and Abednego.

The king asked them, why haven't you bowed like everybody else? I will give you another chance to bow and if you refuse I will cast you at once into the fiery furnace. Shadrach, Meshach, and Abednego told him, "O King, it is not necessary for you to give us another chance, our God will see us through, and even if he does not at this time, we will press on alone with Jesus." Stephen knew what it is to press on alone with Jesus. Standing before the Sanhedrin Council, he rebuked the priest's negative attitude toward the Word of God. Everyone turned against him and started throwing stones at him, but Stephen did not budge, he saw heaven open and Jesus standing on the right hand of God.

Jesus had to press on alone as He paid the price of sin. In the garden of Gethsemane, He took three of His most trusted disciples and told them to pray for Him. He told them, my soul is exceedingly sorrowful, watch with Me for a while. He went back to pray and they fell asleep. Satan pressed the Savior a little harder: Look at them; they cannot even pray with you for a while. Judas, whose feet you have washed, is on his way to betray you. You cannot see your Father's face, so give it up, Jesus. The Savior got nervous and frightened because He could not see the future. Before Him was darker than the darkest night. He could not see beyond the grave, but He continued to make Himself press.

The awful moment had come, the moment that was

Travelling Through Rough Waters

to decide the destiny of this world. The fate of humanity trembled in the balance. Christ, even now, could refuse to drink the bitter cup appointed for guilty man. It was not too late. He could wipe the bloody sweat from his brow and leave man to perish in his sin, but Jesus made Himself press up that Golgotha hill with the cross. If we must run the race and win, we must make ourselves forget anything that can hold us back; we must make ourselves press and we must make ourselves stretch.

Chapter 2

Strength for the Journey

I have decided to write this chapter from three perspectives. I would like to look at strength for the journey from a man's perspective, strength for the journey from a woman's perspective, and strength for the journey from a youth's prospective. Lot, Abraham's nephew, and his family were taken captive in the battle of the four kings. Abraham heard about his nephew and asked God if it was okay to go after the kings and take back his

Travelling Through Rough Waters

nephew. God gave Abraham the green light and he went after them and rescued Lot. Abraham came back and gave God thanks for deliverance; however, sometime after, he started worrying about a return attack by the three kings. Sometimes in life, even when we have done the right thing we worry about it. It is necessary then to have God by our side at all times.

Strength for the Journey from a Man's Perspectives

The Lord came to Abraham one night in a vision and said to him, I am the Lord God, fear not, I asked you to leave your country and I have brought you to this land. I have protected you along the way and I have brought you into this country to possess it. To reinforce the promise, God told Abraham to go outside and look to the heavens, and he saw the unnumbered stars glittering in the heavens, then a voice said to him, "So shall thy seed be."

The patriarch believed God, but he begged for some visible tokens as a confirmation of his faith and that God would be gracious toward him. Abraham said to God, "How do I know that this land will always belong to me and my descendants? Is there some visible evidence you can give me?" Now Abraham had an underlying problem. He was not so much concerned about the land, but he was concerned about this boy that the Lord promised to him. When he said to the Lord, "How do I know that this land will always belong to me and my descendants?" he was alluding to the fact that God was showing him all these stars in the heavens and told him that his descendants would be like the stars, but where was

Strength for the Journey

the boy? Where was the son that was promised? That is what he was trying to say to God and God understood Abraham's feelings, but there was something He needed to do for Abraham's spirituality and He needed to use this promise to get it done. God will come through for you, but He might need to use that particular blessing to do something spiritual for you. We are not the only ones who struggle with our inward thoughts. The Devil presents negative thoughts in our minds sometimes and we worry even though we have the Lord in our lives. Many times faith and reality clash, and it is not because we do not believe in God. The Bible says Abraham was a friend of God, but his mind was disturbed by harassing thoughts that those kings might come back to get him, and the promise God gave him had not come through after twenty years.

God in His mercy tried to comfort him with His promises, just as He has done for us many times, but it seems as if it is just not enough. Abraham pressed God for some tangible evidence. It is not that some of us do not believe in God that we are concerned and sometime even worry, but we cannot see faith the same way we see reality. Reality has a way of dominating our consciousness and sometimes blocks God's goodness and mercy from our sight.

The strength we need to move forward in our spiritual life is a direct link to the throne of mercy, that even in moments of despair and disappointment we will still find strength to go forward. Abraham was struggling, but he was going forward. God said to Abraham, Look up at the twinkling stars in the sky, so shall your seed be. But

Travelling Through Rough Waters

Abraham said, Can you give me a token to prove that you are going to do it? Abraham could not latch on to faith because reality dominated his mind.

We, too, fall into this situation sometimes. We know God, we love God, we believe in God, but reality shakes us up, and we say to God, I know that you are coming, but could I just get a glimpse of your glory while you are coming? Can I get a token to keep me until you come? Depending on where we are in our Christian growth, sometimes He gives us the token and sometime He does not. God condescended to enter into a covenant with Abraham. He said to him, "I will make a covenant with you." I will make a covenant just like the covenant in your culture. The covenant that two people make when they decide to be blood brothers. So go and get yourself a heifer, a female goat, and a ram, each of them must be three years old. Also, bring a dove and a young pigeon. Abraham needed a token and God decided to give him a token of His promise.

The next morning, Abraham got up and brought the animals; he sacrificed them and cut them in half, then placed each half opposite each other. In other words, Abraham cut the animals in half and put one piece on the right and the other piece on the left, so he lined up each half of the animals opposite to each other. He then walked between the pieces, or the halves, and pledged perpetual obedience to God. This is what he did while he walked between the sacrificial offerings. He said, "Let my body be like these [referring to the pieces of meat] or let my body be cut in pieces like these if I break this covenant between me and God."

Strength for the Journey

That is how they made a covenant back then. This covenant process was well known in the land. We saw the same process on Mount Carmel when Elijah summoned the pagan priest to kill a male cow, place it on the altar, and then let their gods respond. If the pagan god responded, he would be the true god, but if Elijah's God responded, He would be the true God. The pagan priest accepted Elijah's proposal because it was a custom among them that they all believed in. God said to Abraham, "Let us make a covenant according to your custom."

After Abraham finished with his part of the vow, he sat down and waited for God to come, respond, and ratify the covenant. He sat there until sunset, keeping the vultures from attacking the carcasses. At sunset the Lord showed up to walk between the carcasses of the animals and to pledge to enter into a covenant relationship with man. As soon as He came on the scene, Abraham fell into a deep sleep. As God pledged the covenant between God and man, Abraham saw a smoking furnace and a burning lamp, symbols of a Divine presence passing between the victims that totally consumed the sacrifices Abraham had set up. God came at sunset. Sometimes Jesus comes for us at sunset. Sometime He comes when it is dark, when we are not expecting Him. His promises are sure and His words are true. Abraham waited from morning until sunset.

He thought the Lord would come at ten a.m., but the Lord did not come. He thought the Lord would come at eleven a.m., but the Lord did not come. He thought the Lord would come at one p.m., but the Lord did not

Travelling Through Rough Waters

come. He thought the Lord would come at three p.m., but the Lord did not come. He thought the Lord would come at five p.m., but the Lord did not come.

The Lord came at sunset. As it was about to get dark, the Lord showed up. Abraham was exhausted from waiting to the point that he fell into a deep sleep. Sometimes you think Jesus will come in the early morning and He does not come. Sometimes you think Jesus will come at noon and He does not come. You wait until three p.m. and still He does not come, and you decide to give up and cast off your trust in Jesus. But how about waiting until sunset? How about waiting until it seems that all hopes are gone, and you are just waiting to see what the end is going to be? Sometimes some of us have already given up. We are just waiting around to see what the end is going to be, and sometimes that is the very time the Lord chooses to make His appearance. When the Lord comes, it is always a very good feeling, all our waiting is forgotten, and joy unspeakable floods our souls. The Lord came and Abraham was fast asleep. While he was sleeping the Lord ratified the covenant with him and gave him a beautiful vision.

Abraham asked God for a token to keep him holding on until the promise came. God showed up and the first thing He did was to change Abraham's name. The second thing He did was to show Abraham the plan of redemption. He showed him the suffering of his posterity and a bird's-eye view of the everlasting establishment of God's people in the promised land. Abraham earned the title "The father of the faithful" because he waited until sunset.

You may say that he fell asleep while he was waiting, but he waited until sunset. You may say that he did not have 20/20 vision because he asked God for a token, but he waited until sunset. You may say that he argued with God about the length of time, and tried to take a short cut by using Ismael for his posterity; nevertheless, he waited until sunset. You may say that after five o'clock he might have wondered if the Lord was still coming, but he waited until sunset. To have strength for the journey, you must wait until sunset.

Strength for the Journey from a Woman's Perspective

Hannah, the wife of Elkanah, also needed strength for the journey, because she too had to wait on the Lord. Hannah was a member of the Shiloh church and a few women in the church made her life miserable, because she could not have children. The Bible said the situation went on for years, and it was worse when the women went to the temple to worship. That means these women went to church to talk about other women. They had this women-thing going on in the church. They did not go to church for a spiritual blessing; they went to discuss the problems of other women in the church.

I Samuel 1:9 tells us that one Sabbath, when they were having lunch, the gossiping got so bad that Sister Hannah got up from the table and burst into tears. Her husband tried to comfort her, but it did not help with her pain. The situation in the church was such that Hannah thought about leaving the church because of all those hypocrites. One day after the family had eaten, she went

Travelling Through Rough Waters

to the prayer room in the temple to pray. We are talking about strength for the journey. The pastor was in his office, as he always was for counseling, but Hannah's problem was bigger than the pastor.

She slipped by the pastor and found a corner where she could pray. She silently cried and prayed at the same time. She told God what some of the women in the church were doing to her. She made a vow to the Lord, "Almighty God, please look down on my misery and help me. Please open my womb and let me bear a son. If you do, I will give him back to you and he will be yours forever" (1 Sam. 1:9-11). The pastor said to her, "How long are you going to stay there trying to attract attention to yourself. You better go home and sleep off your wine because it seems as if you are drunk." She responded to the pastor, I am not the kind of woman you think I am. I have been praying to the Lord. I was telling Him all of my troubles. Let me say a few words to you ladies. For you to survive in the church and carry out your responsibilities, you must remember that wherever you see a group of people, especially women and men too, there is going to be gossiping and trouble of some sort.

I am not making this up; it is biblical. The Bible said some of the women in the Shilo church were picking at Hannah while the preacher was preaching. Some of the women were not even thinking about what the preacher was saying; they were too busy talking about the other women in the church. Ladies, for you to be strong women, you must learn the dynamic of people, particularly those who are like yourself. Leaving the church is not an option. I Samuel 1:9 tells us that the particular problem

Strength for the Journey

in the Shilo church went on year after year. It was not a three-month or six-month problem. It went on year after year. You must resolve in your mind that nobody will ever run you away from God's church. You must say like Job, "Though He slay me yet will I trust Him." You must be resolved in your heart that if I am going to be a blessing in God's church, I must be wise as a serpent and harmless as a dove. I will keep my lips sealed and use my brain. This goes for the men as well. I am sure that when Sister Hannah got up from the table that Sabbath afternoon because of those hypocrites, the Devil told her not to go back to church, but sister Hannah was not about to let anybody run her away from God's church. Ladies, you must learn that when the kitchen gets too hot, you should get out and find an air-conditioned room to cool off. Sister Hannah learned over the years that one of the best ways to resolve her problem, whether they are spiritual or social, was to take them to the Lord in prayer. So she ran to the church and found herself a little corner where she could let it all out and then prayed to the great God of heaven. We are talking about strength for the journey. Sometimes the only thing you can do when people do you wrong is to go to the Lord and cry. Ladies and gentlemen, do not be distracted when others talk about you, particularly if you are innocent. Instead, go to the Lord in prayer. Tell God about your problems and He will fix them for you. If you are doing a job for the church and somebody keeps on talking, do not listen to them. They are being used by the Devil, so just keep on doing what you are doing, don't pay them any attention, they are supposed to be God's children, but Satan

Travelling Through Rough Waters

borrowed some of them.

Do not take things so personally sometimes, because most of the time those who are talking do not know what they are talking about. Sometimes, not even the pastor is in tune with your problem. Eli said to Sister Hannah, "How long are you going to stay there trying to attract attention to yourself?" The pastor is not in tune. This woman is experiencing excruciating psychological pain and she is asking God to help her, and he is talking about drawing attention to herself. Sometimes nobody knows but God; therefore, take it to the Lord in prayer. You must turn your ears from the sounds around you and look unto God who is the author and finisher of your salvation. Ladies, you cannot continue with this women-thing in the church, you must march to the beat of a different drum.

Strength for the Journey from a Youth's perspective

The world has cornered our young adults to the point that some of them have no spiritual spine; but there is no need to give up hope, because there is strength for the journey. I was thinking about my oldest grandson when I was writing this chapter and he inspired me to add strength for the journey from a youth's perspective. Nebuchadnezzar went to Jerusalem and took the Jewish people captive. Among them were some young men, one of whom was Daniel. As soon as Nebuchadnezzar got back to Babylon, he ordered the master of the eunuchs to select from the Jewish captives a group of young men to come to his palace for training. The young men were

Strength for the Journey

to be healthy, handsome, intelligent, self-disciplined, and well-mannered to serve in the royal court. These young men were to be treated as royalty, fed from the same menu of meat and wine as those that were offered to the king. Their training was to last for three years and then the king himself would examine them.

Among those chosen were Daniel, Hananiah, Mishael, and Azariah. All four of these young men were from the tribe of Judah. After they arrived in Babylon, the first thing Nebuchadnezzar did was to change their names—we are talking about strength for the journey. Watch God as He gave these four young men strength for their journey. From the earliest times, psychology has always been a means to accomplish the goals of those who are in authority.

Daniel's name was changed to "Belteshazzar," which means "Bel, protect the king's life." Bel was one of their gods. Hananiah's name was changed to "Shadrach." Mishael's name was changed to "Meshach," and Azariah's name was changed to "Abednego." All of these names identified them as servants of the gods of Babylon. But Daniel and his three friends made up their minds that they were not going to identified with the god of Babylon; instead, they decided to serve the God of heaven. When a person makes up his mind to obey God's word, He will supply him or her with the necessary strength to carry it out. Daniel and his friends resolved not to eat the king's food or drink the king's wine because these were food and drinks that were first offered to idols.

Daniel asked Ashpenaz, who was in charge of the training, to give them the permission to follow their Hebrew

Travelling Through Rough Waters

diet. These young men were captive and they had no right to any special privileges, but because they stood firm for God, He protected them and impressed upon the mind of their trainer to grant them their wishes. Mankind is under God's control, and it does not matter whether you are a child of God or a person of the world. God is ultimately ruler of the universe, so no one can stop God's will. The problem is not whether God has the power to see us through, but whether we have the faith to trust Him to carry us through the dark places of this earth.

Ashpenaz agreed, but kept a close eye to see if these boys' diet was impeding their training. It should not be overlooked, that every opportunity and favor that Daniel and his three friends received from Ashpenaz, was the Lord giving them strength for the journey. Please note also that what Daniel was asking the master of the eunuchs to do was a very serious thing. The master of the eunuchs could be executed if the king knew that he had not carried out his orders, but God can save anybody when he or she does the right thing. After ten days Daniel and his three friends were healthier than the rest of the students, so Ashpenaz allowed them to continue with their diet. Please note that God gives strength for the journey again.

Another point of strength for the journey, God gave Daniel and his three friends insight and skills in whatever subject they had to learn. When the three years of training were over, the master of the eunuchs took all the students to the king, and the king examined them himself and found Daniel and his three friends to be far ahead of all the others. The king was so impressed that he made them permanent members of his court. No matter what question the king asked or what problem he raised, he found them to be ten times better than any of the fortune-tellers and the astrologers who served as his advisers.

To be captured as slaves is one of the worst things that could ever happen to anybody, but when you are a child of God, there is no problem that God cannot handle. If there is a problem, it is not with God, it is with us. Oftentimes, we get nervous and scared, thinking that we are in trouble, but every one of our troubles is God's trouble. These four young men who were taken into captivity could not foresee how they would continue their relationship with God. Many would have given up and complained that there was no way anyone could expect them to survive in such a terrible situation, but whatever the situation the young adult may find himself or herself in, God can give strength for the journey; He can give you strength to overcome your situation.

Chapter 3

Touched by an Angel

The series "Touched by an Angel" has been very successful. It received some of the highest ratings in Hollywood. People are fascinated today with angels. The idea that when a person dies he or she lives again is accepted by many people today, but little do they realized that they are preparing their minds to accept the doctrine of devils. It is said, by the spirit of prophecy that in the last days evil angels will mingle with the children of man to deceive many. Lucifer, the prince of darkness, has decided to throw his little red ball of false doctrine in the pathway of those who are running the race for life everlasting.

It is Satan's most successful and fascinating delusion, one calculated to take hold of the sympathies of those who have laid their loved ones in the grave. Evil angels come in the form of those loved ones and relate incidents connected with their lives, and perform acts that they performed while living. In this way they lead persons to believe that their dead friends are angels, hovering over them and communicating with them. These evil angels who assume to be the deceased friends are regarded with great respect, and with many their word has greater weight than the Word of God." (*Last Day Event*, 161)

By the way, who is this Lucifer who is throwing out his little red balls of false doctrine? There was a time when the universe was in perfect harmony. The angels in heaven served God in love. They carried out their respective responsibilities in harmony and love. The Bible tells us, "One of the angels in heaven (Lucifer by name) interrupted the beautiful harmony and love in heaven." "He was perfect until the day iniquity was found in him" (Ezek. 28:15). This angel is not an ordinary angel; he is wiser than any human being on earth. Ezekiel 28:3 tells us, "Lucifer is wiser than the prophet Daniel."

Ezekiel 28:14 and 17 tells us, "Lucifer is the most beautiful creature that was ever created in the universe." Lucifer was the director of music in heaven. He was able to sing every part of the music at the same time. All the members of the Brooklyn Tabernacle Choir cannot equal to Lucifer when he sings. Lucifer had gotten to the

Travelling Through Rough Waters

place where he wanted to be God (Isa. 14:13-14). But sometimes, if we are not careful, we can find ourselves like Lucifer. In every system on earth you find people like Lucifer who cannot be satisfied with their position, always thinking that they could be better off if they had somebody else's position. We fail to understand that every organization runs better when each participant accepts his or her position and does the best with it.

Because it is God who gives position and talent. Lucifer conspired against God. He decided to overthrow God and take over. It is important to understand the character of this angel who is throwing little red balls in the pathways of those who are running the race of life. The Bible tells us there was war in heaven (Rev. 12:7-9). A literal battle took place in heaven. I do not know what kind of ammunition they used, but according to the Greek a literal battle took place in the dwelling place of God. The Greek word that is used for war is "polemous." The word is always used in reference to a battle going on somewhere.

When people cannot have their way, they will mess things up. They will tell other people that you are bad when they know that it is not true. They will convince others who had no problem with you to think evil of you. Lucifer decided to take on God and the host of heaven. The Bible says, "There is a way that seems right unto a man, but the end thereof are the ways of death" (Prov. 14:12). Our pride will get in the way sometimes. I believe Lucifer said in his mind, I have gotten too far to turn back. Whatever happens I've got to go through with it. A converted man will look into himself and say, Self, you will not get the best of me this time. But sad to say, many of us allow ego and pride to get the best of us. Like Lucifer, some of us will take on anybody we feel we are big enough to fight. "There was war in heaven."

Revelation 12:7 tells us, "There was Polemous in heaven." Michael and the angels fought with the dragon and his angels. Michael, the general of heaven, and his angels fought against the dragon (Lucifer) and his angels, and they were cast out of heaven. All the angels that fell from heaven to the earth are still on the earth today; we call them demons. Revelation 12:4 tells us that Lucifer took one third of all the angels in heaven with him. If you notice, Lucifer has many names:

1. Lucifer (Isa. 14:12)
2. The dragon (Rev. 12:7)
3. The old serpent (Rev. 12:9)
4. The Devil (Rev. 12:9)
5. Satan (Rev. 12:9)

The angels Lucifer took with him from heaven, we call them demons or fallen angels and they are everywhere in the world. They can impersonate human beings. They can look, walk, and talk like any human being whether they are dead or alive. People who tell you that they saw their dead loved ones, they are not completely lying. They saw a spirit or a demon that looks like their departed loved one. The quickness of their eyes deceived their body or their senses. If a demon decided to impersonate a person, you and I cannot tell the difference between your departed loved ones and the demons. Both look

Travelling Through Rough Waters

just the same. Our only safeguard is the scripture. The Bible tells us that when a person dies he does not come back, and he knows nothing, but Lucifer comes along and throws his little red ball of lies. He tells people that their departed loved ones return from the grave in the spirit form and they are watching over living relatives. If you see something look like a person who has departed, you must trust the Word of God and not your senses.

Isaiah 14:12 tells us that Lucifer and his angels came down here and they weaken the nation. Lucifer and these fallen angels are also involved in black magic voodoo. You will see people doing strange things, like walking on nails and hot coals. You should know that there is no such thing. Humans cannot walk on fire and not be burnt. These individuals are working alongside Lucifer and his fallen angels, and the quickness of your eyes deceives your body. No human beings can walk on fire or nails and not respond to the sensation. For anyone to run the race of life successfully, he or she must adhere to sound doctrine. The battle that took place in heaven before mankind was created on planet earth is still raging and Lucifer has not given up. He may not be able to fight with God, but he throws distraction in our way to defeat us on the journey. This subject should be taken seriously, because God hates when His children listen to Lucifer instead of Him. He wiped out a whole nation of people who listened to Lucifer and ignored His command.

In 2 Kings 17:15-18, 23 we read, "The Lord had charged them, that they should not do like them (the heathen) and they left all the commandments of the Lord their God and made them molten images, even two calves, and made a grove and worshiped all the host of heaven and served Baal. And they caused their sons and their daughters to pass through the fire, and used divination and enchantments and sold themselves to do evil in the sight of the Lord, to provoke Him to anger. Therefore, the Lord was very angry with Israel and removed them out of His sight…So was Israel carried away out of their own land to Assyria." Lucifer and his angels are very big on distracting people with divination and enchantments. Come with me to 1 Samuel 28:7-15, Out of desperation Saul (the King of Israel) said to two of his closest officers, "Go and find me a woman who is a spirit medium, I need help…" When they returned they said, "There is a witch at Endor, about eight miles from here." After it was dark Saul disguised himself and went with his two officers to see the woman who lived in the cave. Saul said to her, "Consult the spirits for me. I will give you the name of the man I want to talk to."….The woman said, "Whose spirit do you want me to bring up." Saul said, "Samuel's spirit."

Then the woman went through her incantations and the spirit began to come up….Saul said to the woman, "Tell me what you see." The woman replied, "I see many spirits coming up from the ground and one of them is coming closer." Saul said to the woman, "What does he look like?" the woman answered, "An old man wrapped in a robe." Saul said, "That's Samuel!" and he fell on his knees and bowed with his face to the ground in front of the spirit." Listen to this, "Then the evil spirit impersonating Samuel spoke to Saul, "Why did you bring me back to this land of trouble?" The spirit looked just like

Travelling Through Rough Waters

Samuel and sounded so much like him that Saul believed it really was the prophet…. (*Clear Word Bible*)

When a demon impersonates a person, the counterfeit is perfect. You and I are not able to tell the difference; therefore, we must not trust our senses when a demon is involved. Demons have the ability to do the following:

Talk like our departed loved ones.
Sing like our departed loved ones.
Walk like our departed loved ones.
Smell like our departed loved ones.
Sit like our departed loved ones.
Comb their hair and dress like our departed loved ones.

We cannot trust what we see or hear when it comes to the Devil, the Bible tells us in Ecclesiastes 9:5. "The living knows that they shall die, but the dead knows nothing." If what you see or hear goes contrary to the Word of God, you must not trust your eyes or your senses. Lucifer and these fallen angels present themselves as our departed loved ones, they utter cautions and warnings, which prove to be correct sometimes; but as they gain your confidence they present doctrine that directly undermines your faith in the scriptures. The Devil is a liar, but he does not lie every time. He knows when to lie and he knows when to tell the truth.

Revelation 13:13-14 tells us that Lucifer and these fallen angels have the power to do miracles and deceive people. The dead cannot communicate to the living. The Bible tells us, "The dead knows nothing." So if a spirit comes to you or through the medium of witchcraft, or a psychic reader gives you a message from a departed person, you should not believe it because the Bible tells us that the dead knows nothing. He or she could not be the person who died, because the Bible says the person does not know that he is dead. The voice, words, and appearance may look and sound like your departed loved one, but it is a lie; the Bible tells us that the dead knows nothing. They cannot talk, they cannot sing, they cannot walk, and they cannot move from where they were laid to rest. Do not be fooled by Lucifer's little red ball.

Someone said, Pastor, who could it be? I know what my mother or my daddy looks like. I know their voice. Who could it be but them. Revelation 16:14 tells us that they are the spirits of devils. Demons have the ability to perfectly counterfeit every aspect of our departed loved ones, so don't be surprised if you see something look and talk like somebody you know to be dead. Multitudes are ready to listen to their personal psychic, but have you ever wondered where this information is coming from? How do these people know your business? How do they know that you are going on a trip or your husband or boyfriend is cheating on you? These psychics and witches work with demons and the demons tell them everything.

Demons are also troublemakers and liars. They are always telling others about your business. They try to break up friendships, and they like to start trouble with your friends and your next-door neighbor. There are few who really understand the deceptive power of spiritualism and the dangers of coming under its influence. Many have no real faith in witchcraft and personal psychics, but

Travelling Through Rough Waters

to gratify their curiosity they venture upon forbidden ground and the mighty destroyer exercises his power upon them against their will. He holds them captive and it is only the power of God that can deliver them from Satan's power.

2 Thessalonians 2:10-11 tell us, "Those who do not love the truth, which is their only defense, will be swept away by all kinds of deceptions brought about by the power of evil. Because they have no protection against these delusions, they will end up believing a lie." All who will not believe the Word of God will wind up believing a lie. This is not good news for anybody. When Satan or one of the demons comes to you and lies to you because you do not believe in the Word of God, God will leave you alone to deal with the demons. Many will be confronted by the spirits of devils impersonating departed relatives or friends. These spirits will appeal to our sympathies. They will work miracles to win our confidence, but you must be prepared to withstand them with the Word of God: "The dead know nothing and if you see anyone looking like your departed loved one, most likely it is the spirit of the Devil. Even when we pray, demons are standing by to throw off the work of God. Right now there are demons trying to discourage you and tell you not to listen to what you are reading, that the author is not telling the truth; but don't you be afraid. God has sent powerful angels from heaven to protect you and author who wrote this book.

Let me shake you up a little. Right now many of us are getting very comfortable with spiritualism in our home. Satan is getting our minds ready to believe that when a person dies he can come back and do good deeds for the community or our fellow man. In many TV series, beautiful people who are dead walk around doing good things for others people; thus many people get comfortable with the idea that the dead help out those who are living. But the Bible says the dead know nothing, they do not know that they are dead. Satan has taken the lie, which he told to Eve, right to you and I through the television. He lied to Eve through a beautiful snake and he is lying to us through our beautiful television set. Isaiah 8:19 tells us, "When they shall say unto you, seek unto them that have familiar spirits, and unto wizards that peep and that mutter [about the future], should not a people seek unto their God? Why should the living go to the dead?"

Lucifer wants to control this world, but every now and then he has to sit down and consider the end. Ezekiel 28:12-14 reminds him how things used to be in heaven. He was the model of perfection, full of wisdom and beauty. He was the anointed cherub, but his heart was lifted up because of his beauty and wisdom and he wanted to control this world. But I know that Christ is coming someday to claim this world as His. Michael, the archangel, threw Lucifer out of heaven, and He is coming back to take planet earth from him.

Lucifer knows full well that planet earth belongs to the Creator, Jesus Christ, because He died and paid the price for it. And it won't be long before He comes to claim what truly belongs to Him. Lucifer's only hope is to keep people on planet earth in darkness, keep throwing his little red balls of distraction at us so that we will

Travelling Through Rough Waters

be distracted and not be saved. Lucifer knows that God will make all things new. Lucifer has made a huge mess down here, but Christ will come and make all things new again. Everything around us sometimes seems so confusing, but the Bible has the answer. God will make all things new.

Time is running out for many of us. Satan's plan is to take us all to hell, but Jesus has promised a home in glory, and time is running out for a lot of us. Behold, He stands at the door knocking; if any man hears His voice and opens up the door of his heart, He will come in. Jesus promises us a crown of life, and Lucifer promises us fame and fortune—which one will you take today?

Chapter 4

What in Hell Do You Want?

Most people who are running the race for life or traveling on the old ship of Zion are running from hell, but there are some people who don't seem to care. Their attitude about hell is like that of Lot's sons-in-law. Archaeologists dug the earth and found remains of people who died in the fire of Sodom and Gomorrah. Lot pitched his tent toward Sodom (Gen. 13:13), but the men of Sodom were wicked. The sins of Sodom went

Travelling Through Rough Waters

up to heaven and God decided to destroy the city. One evening about sunset two men approached the city gate. These men were angels of the Lord. They told Lot to escape to the mountain.

God never punishes anyone without sending him or her some type of warning. God is kind, loving, and fair (Gen. 19:17). The angels told Lot to escape for his life. Do not look back (Gen. 19:14). Lot went and told his daughters and sons-in-law to leave the city because the judgment of the Lord was coming, but they mocked him. Lot delayed for a while, because he was trying to convince his children, and the angels took him by the hands and led him away from the city (Gen. 19:24). Then the Lord rained upon Sodom and upon Gomorrah brimstone and fire.

The angel told them not to look back, but Lot's wife looked back and she became a pillar of salt (Gen. 19:26). Sodom and Gomorrah is used by God as an example of the destruction of the wicked in future judgment. Those who live ungodly shall not escape God's Judgment. In 2 Peter 2:6, it says, God turned the city of Sodom and Gomorrah into ashes. Some people said God is too merciful to burn anybody in hellfire. Well, how about letting God speak for Himself. Does God's love stop him from burning people in hellfire? Is it unloving to burn people in hellfire? In Matthew 13:41-43 we read, "So shall it be in the end of the world, the Son of Man shall send His angels and they shall gather them which do iniquity and shall cast them into a furnace of fire." Everyone who continues to do iniquity will be burned in hellfire. By the way, what is iniquity? Iniquity is the absence of moral or spiritual values, injustice, unfairness, wickedness, dishonesty, disrespectfulness, sexual immorality, unrighteousness—just to mention a few. So would it be safe to say anybody who will not stop lying, anybody who will not stop being dishonest, anyone who continues to devise evil plans for his brother or sister, anyone who continues to practice sexual immorality, anyone who continues to be unfair in his dealing or business practices with other people, anyone who is unrighteous and continues to be unrighteous will be burned in hell. Now, I mentioned previously that I am a Biblical Reporter, so please do not accuse me of sending anybody to hell, I am trying to dissect Matthew 13:41-43. Jesus said at the end of the world He will send His angels to gather them that do iniquity and cast them into hellfire. When we look up the word "iniquity," we learn that to do iniquity is to be an immoral person, an unspiritual person, an unjust person, an unrighteous person, an unfair person, a dishonest and disrespectful person, and a sexually immoral person. We conclude then that regardless of how loving God is, people who do iniquity and do not change cannot go to heaven with the Son of Man, and there is no in-between ground; if you do not go to heaven, you will be going to hell.

John the Revelator even takes this thing a little further, and my dissection of Matthew 13: 41-43 seems to be right on target. John did not beat around the bushes as to who will be going to hell. He described those who will be in hellfire if they do not change. In Revelation 21:8 he said, the fearful and the unbelievers, the abominable, the murderers, and the whoremongers, the sorcerers or

Travelling Through Rough Waters

witches or psychics, the adulterers and the liars. These are the people John said you can expect see in hellfire. I also believe that a couple church people are going to be there too.

How long will these people burn in hellfire? Some people believe that they will burn forever. They cite Revelation 20:10, where John said the wicked will burn in hell forever. Forever in the Bible can be literally translated "until the end of the age" or as long as he shall live. According to Malachi 4:1-3, the wicked will turn into ashes. They will be consumed, burned up, and turned into ashes. The old age of sin and death is ended. God ushers in a new age. Revelation 21:1-4 tells us, God will create a new heaven and a new earth. There will be no more crying, no more death, no more sickness, no more pain, and there will be no more burning. The term forever was used frequently in the Old Testament, but it means as long as the subject lives.

In Exodus 21:6, the slave was to serve his master forever, but the slave did not live forever—he finally died; so therefore, the statement had to mean until the slave died. In 1 Samuel 1:22 Hannah told her husband that she would take Samuel to the temple and he would served the Lord forever, but Samuel did not live forever. In both of these instances the time period was as long as they lived. When the word forever refers to God's creatures on planet earth, it can only refer to a period of time, because people on planet earth do not live forever. They live until they die. The people who will burn in hell, will burn until they die. Malachi 4:1-3 says they will turn into ashes.

What in Hell Do You Want?

There are some people who will be burned in hellfire who are already dead, so where are these people now. Purgatory is a Roman Catholic teaching. According to the Church, there are some people who die who are not spiritually ready for heaven, so they go to purgatory, a place of purification or a place of temporary punishment so that they can be made ready (according to the idea, these people should die in a state of grace). Another point to note, these people who are in temporary punishment, some of them are there for hundreds of years. This is a very long time for God to punish people. This punishment is worse than the literal burning; however, I think that most Catholics would like the benefit of this idea, because in this case, most Catholics, if not all, would go to heaven. They could live, not worrying about eternity, and when they die, if things were not right with their soul, they could fix it in purgatory.

Malachi 4:1-3 tells us that in the literal burning, people will burn to ashes and it does not take hundreds of years for anybody to burn to ashes. Another point to note with purgatory, these people are not dead. A dead person cannot repent or change for the better. For these people to be in a place of purification, they have to have some type of cognition so that they can become better to go to heaven. This doctrine also clashes with Luke 16: 26 where Jesus tells the story about the rich man and Lazarus. In the story He spoke about a gulf, "There is a great gulf fixed." There is a great distance between heaven and hell—hell refers to the grave—so no one from here can go down there nor anyone from there can come up here.

Travelling Through Rough Waters

In Luke 16:19-31, Jesus tells a story from Jewish folklore about a rich man and a poor man to make a point. According to the story, there were two men; one was rich and the other was poor. The poor man had open sores and he sat at the rich man's gate every day begging food. The rich man never told him to leave, but he just ignored him. The poor man finally died and was carried by the angels to Abraham's lap (or into glory). Soon afterward, the rich man also died and was buried. According to the story, the rich man looked up out of hell where he was in awful pain and saw the poor man sitting in glory next to Abraham. The rich man cried out to Father Abraham and asked him to send the poor man down with a little sip of water to cool his tongue because it was very hot in hell. Abraham told the rich man that the poor man could not bring him the water because there was a great gulf fixed between them, so that no one can go down to him and no one can come from him to where he and the poor man were.

There is a great gulf fixed so that no one can come from me to you and from you to me. In other words, there is no communication between the living and the dead. Everything should be fixed before you and I depart from this world. The word "gulf" here represents the difference in moral character between the rich man and Lazarus. There is a big difference between Lazarus's Christ-like character and the rich man's character. Our character makes the difference. Many of us look just alike. We go to church every week and participate in church activities, but our characters are far from being pure. This one aspect of our being makes the difference in where we spend our eternity.

The word "fixed" also makes reference to the fact that after death our character cannot be changed. It is fixed forever. So if you die an unrighteous person, you will rise up from the grave an unrighteous person; there is no change in the grave. Job 21:30-32 tells us, "The wicked is reserved to the day of destruction...Yet shall he be brought to the Grave and shall remain in the Tomb." Purgatory is a doctrine taught by the Catholic Church. It means, "to make clean, to purify." According to the Catholic teaching, it is a place or condition of temporary punishment for those who have departed this life and are not entirely free from faults, or have not fully paid the satisfaction due to their transgressions. Jesus and Job seem to contradict the purgatory doctrine. Jesus and Job said when a person dies his destiny is fixed forever.

What about hell? Is it burning someplace on the earth now and waiting for its victims? According to 2 Peter 2:4 there is no hell burning anywhere at this time; hell is in the future. Peter said, the angels who sinned in heaven, God cast them out and they are being reserved until the Day of Judgment, so not even the demons who were cast out of heaven, as wicked as they are, are burning anywhere, they are waiting until the last day. According to the Bible, the final destruction of the wicked comes at the end of time. The fire of hell originates from heaven at the end of time.

There are no hot spots in the earth at this time that are called hell. Revelation 20:9 tells us that the wicked went upon the breath of the earth and compassed.

Travelling Through Rough Waters

The camp of the saints about and the beloved city and fire came down from God out of heaven and devoured them. Where are the wicked now who have already died? John 5:28-29 tells us that they are in the grave. God takes care of everybody at the same time. Some people are so terrible, you would think that they need to be in hell a little longer than others, but God does not see as man sees.

There are times some ministers will try to comfort the bereaved by telling them that their departed loved ones are in heaven, but there is no such thing. This is what the Word of God says: "Jesus died and rose again; therefore, those who died believing in Him will be raised to life by God just as Jesus was raised. We are telling you this by the authority of the Lord Jesus Christ...we who are still alive when He comes will not be taken to heaven ahead of our loved ones who have died in Christ and are now sleeping. When Christ descends from heaven....He will give a shout of command, the trumpet call of God to the dead and the dead in Christ will rise first, then those believers living at that time will be changed and together with those who have been resurrected will be caught up in the sky to meet the Lord in the air, and from then on we will all be with the Lord" (I Thess. 4:13-17).

The text is very clear. The saints who died are sleeping in their grave. All of God's people go to heaven together. If you notice in I Thessalonians 4:13-17, God did not bring any saints with Him from heaven, He called all the dead saints from the grave.

If you also notice, the people who are going to hell did not get up out of their grave when God called the saints. In 1 Thessalonians 4:16, it tells us that the saints rise first, which means there is another resurrection after the saints. Revelation 20:5 tells us when the other resurrection took place. It says, "They had not received the mark (talking about the saints who were previously raised from the dead). They were all there and shared judgment with Christ for a thousand years. All of them had been raised at the first resurrection, but the wicked remained dead and were not resurrected until these thousand years were over." So, there you have it, everyone who died are in their grave sleeping; it makes no difference if you are a saint or a wicked person, every one stays in their grave until Christ calls them from the grave.

What Will Happen When the Wicked Are Raised from the Grave?

John the Revelator had a vision about this very subject. You can read about it in Revelation 20:7-14, but let me sum it up for you. At the end of the thousand years, God set Satan free and He raised up the wicked dead. When Satan saw all the wicked people from all nations and from all ages, the number of the wicked could not be counted, they were like the sand on the seashore. The earth was filled with wicked people. Satan sprang into action and persuaded them to join him in a battle against the City of God, which had just come down from heaven. The wicked listened to him and, under his leadership, surrounded the beautiful city where the saints were, and as they launched their attack, fire came down from God out of heaven and consumed them all.

Before they were destroyed, John said that he saw a

Travelling Through Rough Waters

great white throne. The form of the One who sat on it was so radiant that the earth and the sky seemed to flee from His very presence, but there was no place for man to hide. Then all the wicked who had been resurrected, whether they had been great or small, stood together with Satan in front of the One who sat on the throne. The Book of Life was opened and the Book of Death was open. Then the lives of the wicked were replayed before them and before the universe, and they understood why they were not allowed to live, for they were judged according to what they had done as recorded in the books.

Everyone who had ever lived was there—those who had been buried at sea as well as those who had been buried on land. All were present to hear the final word from the One who sat on the throne. This was the great judgment, and all were judged the same way. Everyone bowed before the throne and acknowledged that God's ways were best, and that He was a just God. Then fire came down out of heaven and in mercy God ended their lives. Death and the grave also came to an end with this fire. This total extinction by the lake of fire is the second death. This same fire also cleansed the earth.

Anyone whose name was not recorded in the Book of Life was consumed by the lake of fire. Because of God's justice and mercy, it is impossible to save the sinner in his sin, so He deprives him of his existence, which he has proven himself unworthy to have. David said in Psalm 37:10, that the wicked shall be as if they have not been. We started out this chapter by asking the question, "What in hell do you want?" What is it that made hell so attractive to people? John tells us in Revelation 20:8 that the wicked who will be burned in hellfire were like the sand on the seashore. This statement indicates that the people who will be going to hell cannot be counted. Who have you ever seen trying to count the grains of sand on the seashore?

John also said in the same passage that the earth will be filled with the wicked. In the King James Version, it says, "And he shall go out to deceive the nations, [speaking of Satan] which are in all four quarters of the earth." Now, just think with me for a while; the total surface of the earth is about 197 million square miles (509 million square kilometers), for the wicked to take up the space of 197 million square miles on the earth (each man occupying just about 36 inches when standing before God on the judgment day), there has to be something about hell that draws people to it. There are many signs to deter people from going to hell, but it seems as if the signs of the coming danger only pick up the momentum of the people going to hell. There are some stormy times before us and around us. The world is stirred with the spirit of war. The world is becoming more and more lawless. Nations are against nations; there is no doubt that the tensions between these nations will not cease anytime soon. Not to mention these tensions only get more intensified as the destiny of planet earth draws near.

In quick succession we see fire and flood, earthquake, terrorist activities, war and bloodshed around the world. Something is about to happen real soon. It should be noted that God never let people go into captivity or

Travelling Through Rough Waters

destruction without sending some kind of warning, and those who had faith in His word and acted out their faith in obedience to His command escaped the coming doom. Noah was told, "Come thou and all thy house into the Ark for thee only have I found righteous before me" (Gen. 7:1). Noah obeyed and was saved from the flood that destroyed the antediluvian world. The angels told Lot, "Up, get you out of this place" (Gen. 19:14). Lot placed his faith in God and under the guidance of the angels he was saved from the fire that destroyed Sodom and Gomorrah. Jesus told His disciples about the destruction that would come upon Jerusalem. He told them to look for the signs of the coming doom.

The disciples watched for the signs and fled Jerusalem before the Romans destroyed the city in AD 70. There are warning signs for us to run from the final destruction that is coming upon this world, but the prediction of the escapee does not look good. John the Revelator pointed out that of all that happens in the past, nothing really changes. I wish the prediction of the escapee was more positive. I wish I had a better report to give, but sad to say, nothing really changes. People love the things that make them go to hell. May the great God of heaven help you and me to pay close attention to the warning signs and run the other direction from hell.

Chapter 5

The Seven Last Plagues

The seven last plagues is a subject that a lot of people do not fully understand, but we all should seek to understand this subject because it is an issue that will affect all mankind on the earth. A clear understanding of the order of events preceding Christ's return is vital. Romans 13:11 tells us, "Considering the time we are living in, it's high time for us to wake up, because our lives might end sooner than we think." If it was important for

Travelling Through Rough Waters

us to continue our relationship with God through Jesus Christ when we first became believers, it's much more important now. The Bible teaches that Jesus will return to this earth in the near future, but there are some events that will take place before he comes. Having an understanding of these last day events before Christ actually shows up on planet earth is vital. If we know the order of things that will be taking place before He comes, we could make a more intelligent decision in regard to our eternity.

The Book of Revelation talks about "the seven last plagues"—what are they and when will these plagues fall on the earth, and how will they affect the earth and the people on the earth. As your Biblical Reporter I would like to take you along with me as I go and dig to find answers to the questions proposed.

What Are the Seven Last Plagues

According to the Bible, the seven last plagues are the wrath of God. This is what Revelation 15:7 says: "And one of the four beasts gave unto the seven angels seven golden vials full of the wrath of God." I like the way the Clear Word Bible says it: "Before the angels left for planet earth, one of the four living beings standing by the throne of God handed each of the seven angels a golden bowl. Each bowl was filled with one of the seven last plagues. These plagues will demonstrate the anger of our eternal God against sin." So let us establish the fact that the seven last plagues is the wrath of God upon mankind and planet earth.

The Seven Last Plagues

When Will the Seven Last Plagues Fall Upon Mankind and Upon the Earth?

First of all, it should be noted that when the seven last plagues start falling, the probation of planet earth will be closed. John alluded to this fact in Revelation 15:5, where he said he saw the tabernacle of the testimony in heaven was open, indicating that no one was ministering in the Most Holy place.

The earthly tabernacle gives us the key to this verse. In the earthly tabernacle there was a vale that divided the holy place from the Most Holy place. The priest would go behind the vale once a year to minister for the people. The ark of the testimony was in the Most Holy place and above the ark of the testimony was the Shekinah glory or the presence of God and the priest ministered before God for the people. What the priest did back in the biblical days was an example of what Christ does in heaven for us today, but John said he got a glimpse into the Most Holy place and no one was there, it was open, indicating that Christ's priestly ministry in heaven was over when the seven last plagues started falling upon the earth. Christ stands before God the Father and litigates the case of all who accept Him as their personal savior. As long as there is a case to be litigated, Christ will be there, and when His work is finished, the probation for mankind will be over. John said during the time of the plagues, he looked into the Most Holy place and Christ was not there.

In Revelation 15:8 John reemphasized that when the angels were on earth carrying out God's destructive work upon sin and sinners, no human being was in the

Travelling Through Rough Waters

sanctuary. The emphasis on "human being in the sanctuary" is pointing to Jesus who is a part of the human family, because he is the Son of God and He is also the Son of man. I pointed out previously that when God sends His angels to do His destructive work upon sin and sinners, probation on planet earth will be closed. But what is this probation that will be closed? Everybody on planet earth has time to make things right with God. And I do not care who you are; if you are a Christian, a Muslim, or a Buddhist, you will have to face God one day. God has set a day to judge the world and if you are a citizen of this world, you shall be judged one day (Acts 17:31). So there is a time for every man to make things right with God in regard to his soul's salvation and when that time is past, your time to make thing right with God will be past, and there is no second chance in the judgment of God and there is no appeal.

God looks at every man's case individually and when he makes a decision on your case, your probation is closed. Your destiny has been decided. One songwriter writes, "The Judgment has set, the books have been opened, how shall we stand in that great day, when every thought and word and action, God, the righteous Judge, shall weigh? O, how shall we stand that moment of searching, when all our sins those books reveal? When from that court, each case decided, shall be granted no appeal? How shall we stand in that great day? How shall we stand in that great day? Shall we be found before Him wanting? Or with our sins all washed away?"

The First Angel

John said he heard a voice out of heaven saying to the angels who had just left heaven with the plagues, "Go your way and pour out the vials of the wrath of God upon the earth" (Rev. 16:1). So the first angel poured out his bowl on the land and the people who had agreed to receive the mark of the beast and who were worshiping the image of the beast broke out with irritating and painful sores all over their bodies. Who is this beast? We will look at this beast separately in another chapter. The first angel poured out his vial, or bowl, upon the earth and painful sores broke out on people. It was not just one or two sores on the body; there were sores all over the body. You do not want to receive the mark of the beast. John said these sores were falling on people who received the mark of the beast (Rev. 16:2).

This is not a joke, this happened before in Egypt. God told Pharaoh to let His people go and Pharaoh decided that he was not going to listen to God and God sent ten plagues onto the Egyptians. Each time He sent another plague, it was worse than the previous one. Keep in mind that there will be no place to buy pain medication or antibiotics.

The pharmacies will be closed because all the employees, including the doctors, have sores over their bodies and no medication or antibiotic can stop this pain. Hospitals will be overflowing with people seeking emergency care, schools will be closed, and businesses will be closed because employees are sick. There will be a halt in construction of businesses and the making of automobiles, but God's people will be safe. Psalm 46:1-3 tells us,

Travelling Through Rough Waters

"God is our refuge and strength, a very present help in trouble. Therefore, we will not fear, though the earth be removed, and though the mountains be carried into the midst of the sea, though the water thereof roars and is troubled, though the mountains shake with the swelling thereof."

The Second Angel
The second angel quickly followed the first angel and poured out his bowl on the oceans of the world, and the water stopped moving, because it had become stagnant and red as the blood of a dead man, and every creature in the sea died. About 71 percent of the earth is covered with water, and even though all the oceans are connected in some way, most often the world is divided into four major oceans: the Pacific Ocean, the Atlantic Ocean, the Arctic Ocean, and the Indian Ocean. Some say there are five oceans, the fifth being an ocean surrounding Antarctica called the Antarctic Ocean or the Southern Ocean. When the second angel pours out his bowl, all five of the world's oceans will turn into blood. Notice that the Bible says the blood was like the blood of a dead man (Rev. 16:3). The blood of a dead man is not the same as regular blood of a living person. When a person dies, his blood coagulates and becomes thick. The creatures in the sea died because they could not live in blood. So while the people are suffering from the sores on their bodies, another epidemic strikes, and the water turns into blood. How bad can it get, for you to have sores all over your body and, to make matters worse, you cannot find water to wash your wound? So

the people are hurting, with no water to bathe in, and there is a terrible odor coming from all the oceans of the world. Everybody in the world smells the same odor and has the same sores except for the people of God.

The Third Angel
John said the third angel quickly followed and poured out his bowl on the springs and rivers of the earth and all of them turned into blood. John said that he heard the angels were saying that God was just in giving the wicked blood to drink. There are 165 major rivers in the world and thousands of other rivers that have never been counted. Michigan is a state in the US, with a total of 97,990 square miles, and this area alone has over 300 rivers. The third angel poured out his bowl on the rivers and all the rivers of the world turned into blood. So the people went to the pipe in the kitchen and blood came out of it. They went to the bathroom to bathe and blood came out of it.

Let us take a quick look. The plague from the first angel has not subsided and the second and third angels come in quick succession and inflict more plagues on the people. People are still suffering from the sores, they have to deal with the odor from the oceans, and now on top of it all they have to drink blood to quench their thirst. Revelation 16:6 says, "For they have shed the blood of the saints and the prophets, and God has given them blood to drink." No one should ever receive the seven last plagues; I am going to do whatever it takes to be on the Lord's side, because this is not good. This prediction sounds like a fairy tale, but please do not take it lightly.

Travelling Through Rough Waters

God's words always come through. This prediction will be fulfilled on planet earth. The Bible says if you hear my voice, harden not your heart. Isaiah 33:16 tells us that God's people will be safe during the time of the plagues. The righteous will not have to worry, their bread and water will be sure. When the plagues had fallen onto Egypt, the people of God were living in Goshen and none of the plagues dared to enter the land of Goshen. The Lord knows how to deliver His own. Not one of God's people needs to worry about drinking blood when the seven last plagues are falling.

The Fourth Angel
Revelation 16:8 tells us, the fourth angel poured out his vial upon the sun, and power was given to the sun to scorch man. Some people may underestimate former Vice President Al Gore's theory on global warming, but planet earth is now preparing herself for the fourth plague, or the fourth angel. In 1936, temperatures soared in Texas to 120 degrees Fahrenheit. Death Valley, California, recorded the world's highest temperature at 128 degrees Fahrenheit. People were cautioned to stay away from this extreme temperature, but there will be nowhere to hide from the fourth plague. The sun will unleash its power upon those who received the mark of the beast.

So let us recap thus far. While the people are suffering from the sores on their bodies, another epidemic strikes, and the water turns into blood. The people are hurting, with no water to bathe in and a terrible odor coming from all the oceans of the world. The third angel quickly follows and pours out his bowl on the springs and rivers of the earth and all of them turn into blood. Now, to make matters worse, there is no water to drink or, if you are thirsty enough, you will have to drink the blood. The angels do not give people a break. The fourth angel pours out his bowl upon the rays of the sun. The rays, behaving like an individual, respond to the command and intensify their power and burn people so severely that they think they are on fire, but the people do not repent; they curse God because of their pain and refuse to admit that what they did was wrong (Rev. 16:11).

God's people will be safe on the earth. In that day, inanimate objects will behave like animate ones. The heat will know whose skin to scorch and whose skin not to scorch. David looked down the ages and saw the saints during this time and penned the words in Psalm 91:1-5: "He who dwells in the sacred place of the Most High will find rest in the shadow of the Almighty. I will say of the Lord, 'He is my refuge and fortress, my God, the One I trust.' He will deliver you from Satan's trap and from the deadly disease of sin. He will cover you with His feathers and hide you under His wings. His truth will defend and protect you. Do not be afraid of the enemy who attacks at night, nor of his arrows that fly by day."

Where Is the Dwelling Place of the Most High That David Spoke About?

David said, "He that dwelleth in the secret place of the Most High shall abide under His shadow." In other words, anyone who has an intimate relationship with God can be at rest. It does not matter how intense our fear of

Travelling Through Rough Waters

the coming danger may be—we can be at rest. This is true, but we must believe it for it to work. Oftentimes for us to have this kind of faith in God, we must ignore some of what we see with our eyes and some of what we understand with our minds, because oftentimes faith and reality do not run parallel. It is paradoxical to tell me that the light and power man is coming to turn my light off, and he finally comes and turns the light off, then you tell me don't worry about it, you've got light because the Almighty God is your protector.

Some people will have problems with this kind of reasoning; but according to the bible, Christians are a unique group of people. They are God's children and they have transcended the boundaries of the human domain into a realm that only the eyes of faith can dwell. Someone said, "Pastor, God is asking me to do something that I cannot do." God is in the process of making you and me into soldiers of the cross. Now, these special blessings only come to those who make their dwelling place in God. The child who claims by words that he dwells in God will likely to find himself among the rest. These promises are for the faithful followers of God. According to Psalm 91:9, the righteous are protected because he has made the Lord his dwelling place, and the Most High God his habitation. So where is this dwelling place of God that David is talking about in this passage of scripture? Let us see if we can figure it out together.

Your dwelling place is where you live.
Your dwelling place is where you sleep.
Your dwelling place is where you eat.
Your dwelling place is where you socialize.

The Seven Last Plagues

Your dwelling place is where you study.
Your dwelling place is where the family counsels together.
Your dwelling place is where you pray.
So we conclude that David is saying here:
If you live with God,
If you eat with God,
If you sleep with God,
If you socialize with God,
If you study with God,
If you counsel with God,

If you pray to God, there is no need to worry when trouble comes because God cohabitated with you. Jesus was sleeping in the boat while the storm was raging, because he was dwelling in the secret place of the Most High. When the mad men from the graveyard charge down the mountainside after Jesus and the disciples, the disciples ran, but Jesus stood His ground because He was dwelling in the secret place of the Most High.

The Fifth Angel

Revelation 16:10 tells us the fifth angel followed quickly and poured out his bowl on the seat of the beast or the headquarters of the beast, and his kingdom was plunged into darkness. The beast here represents primarily the papacy in its revived state, not so much in its religious aspect as in its assumed role as a world power. This is the same beast we saw in Revelation 13:1-5 and Satan gave him power, his seat, and great authority. Except for the small remnant that still resists the beast's supremacy,

Travelling Through Rough Waters

Satan numbered the world as his subject and it is through the revived papacy in particular that he seeks to secure undisputed control over the entire human race (Ellen G. White, The Great Controversy, p.571-656, Testimony, Vol. 5, p.472)

Darkness upon the kingdom of the Beast

This beast is doing something that he should not be doing, because the seven last plagues came right after the beast and the people who worship the beast and his image. I do hope as we read, we are observing the words that are being used, so that we can have insight into this deep subject. Revelation 16:2 says, the first angel poured out his bowl on the people who had agreed to receive the mark of the beast and worship the image that the beast set up. So from the get-go, we can see that this conflict is over worship that belongs to God, and the beast, through some scheme, is trying to take the worship that belongs to God. We will look at the beast and his activities when we get to the subject on the mark of the beast.

The Greek implies that this darkness was a literal darkness and it remained for a period of time. If you ever study the ten plagues of Egypt, you will notice that one of the plagues was darkness, so it is not unusual to see darkness being used as one of the seven last plagues. The darkness in Egypt was so thick that a person could actually feel the darkness (Exod. 10:21). We know that the people realized that these plagues came from God, because they cursed God for sending the plagues, but they still refused to recognize God's authority and repent of their sin. Christians should not be surprised at the hostility and hardness of the hearts of unbelievers. Even when the power of God is fully and completely revealed, many will still refuse to repent. If you find yourself ignoring God more and more, turn back to Him before your heart becomes too hard to repent.

The Sixth Angel

Revelation 16:12 tells us the sixth angel quickly followed and poured out his bowl on the great river Euphrates and her many canals and immediately the water dried up so that the way of the king of the east might be prepared. There are two views on the "drying up of the river Euphrates." According to the first view, "the great river Euphrates" represents the Ottoman Empire, and the drying up of the river is the gradual dissolution of that empire. "The king of the east" is the nations of the Orient, and "Armageddon" is the literal valley of Megiddo in northern Palestine; thus, the dissolution of the Ottoman Empire is seen as preparing the way for the Oriental nations to join battle with those of the West in the valley of Megiddo.

According to the second view, "the great river Euphrates" represents people (please be aware that in prophecy, water represents people—Rev. 17:15) over whom mystical Babylon holds sway. The drying up of its water is the withdrawal of people support from Babylon. The king of the east represents Christ and those who accompany Him, and Armageddon is the last battle of the great controversy between Christ and Satan being fought out on the battlefield on this earth; thus the

Travelling Through Rough Waters

withdrawal of human support from mystical Babylon is seen as the removal of the last barrier to her ultimate defeat and punishment.

The two views have a lot in common. Both views believed that the last great battle of earth's history is still in the future and it is the great day of God Almighty. Both views believed that the great river Euphrates is symbolic of human beings and the three unclean spirits that are seen in the six plagues represent the papacy, apostate Protestantism, and spiritualism. Both views also believed that this battle will be a real battle with real people employing real weapons, all the nations of the earth will be involved, and Christ and the armies of heaven will intervene and bring the battle to an end (SDA Bible Commentary, Vol. 7, 842-843).

The sixth plague strikes directly at Satan and the papacy, and activates the closing phase of earth's history. The activity of the sixth plague runs into the Second Coming of Christ. It is Christ who brings to an end the final battle that the sixth plague prepared the world to enter. It is safe to say that the probation of the world will be closed before the seven last plagues fall. If the seven last plagues bring to an end the destiny of mankind, earth's probation has to be closed before the angels leave heaven. It is important to note that none of God's people will die in this battle against the righteous.

E.G. White tells us in *Early Writings*, p. 283: That the people were at liberty after a certain time to put them (the saints) to death, but in this hour of trial the saints were calm and composed, trusting in God and leaning upon His promise that a way of escape would be made

The Seven Last Plagues

for them. In some places before the time for the decree to be executed, the wicked rushed upon the saints to slay them, but angels in the form of man of war fought for them. Satan wished to have the privilege of destroying the saints of the Most High, but Jesus bade His angels watch over them.....Next came the multitude of the angry wicked, and next a mass of evil angels, hurrying on the wicked to slay the saints, but before they could approach God's people, the wicked must first pass this company of mighty holy angels. This was impossible. The angels of God were causing them to recede and also causing the evil angels who were pressing around them to fall back.

The Seventh Angel

Revelation 16:17-21 tells us, quickly the seventh angel followed the sixth angel and poured out his bowl into the earth's atmosphere, then the One who sat on the throne spoke and said, "It is done!" At this time, all across the sky were flashes of lighting, followed by loud peals of thunder. There was a tremendous earthquake, stronger than any earthquake since the creation of mankind. It was so severe that the entire planet shook. The earthquake struck with such force that entire islands disappeared, and large mountains simply dropped out of sight. The earthquake was followed by a global hailstorm with each hailstone weighing about one hundred pounds. It was so terrible that the people cursed God. When the plagues were over, the earth looked like a wilderness.

There is something I don't want you to miss. Revelation

Travelling Through Rough Waters

16:19 says, "And the great city was divided into three parts." Which city is this? It should be noted that this statement is not talking about a normal city as we know it to be, but a special city or something that is of interest to the plagues. Revelation 17:18 gives us some insight: "And the woman which thou saw is that great city which reigns over the kings of the earth." Let us take another glimpse from a different prospective. I will read it from the *Clear Word Bible*: "They will stand back in amazement and fear and will say to each other, 'Oh no! Our great city, this global Babylon that we have built, this mighty city has lost all her wealth in only one prophetic hour.'" (Rev. 18:10). Now, a day in prophecy equals one year (Ezek. 4:6 and Num. 14:34), so an hour would equal to about two weeks to less then a month. I would think that the prophet John was focusing on the rapid destruction of this great spiritual Babylon that styled herself as a great city. This great union between the Dragon, the Beast, and the false prophets came to a crashing end. The union lost its cohesion and split up into three separate parts.

Let us do a final recap

The first angel poured out his bowl and there were sores all over people's bodies. While the people were suffering from the sores on their bodies, another epidemic struck. The second angel poured out his bowl on the oceans and the water turned into blood. So now the people were hurting, with no water to bathe in, and there was a terrible odor coming from all the oceans of the world. The third angel quickly followed and poured out his bowl on the springs and rivers of the earth and

The Seven Last Plagues

all of them turned into blood. Now, to make matters worse, there was no water to drink or, if you were thirsty enough, you would have to drink the blood. The angels did not give the earth a break. The fourth angel poured out his bowl upon the rays of the sun, and the rays of the sun start behaving like an individual responding to a command, and intensified their temperature and burned people so severely that they cursed God because of their pain, but they refused to admit that what they had done was wrong. (Revelation 16:11). So now, the people have sores, no water to drink and wash their sores, and now this unbearable heat from the fourth angel.

The fifth angel poured out his bowl on the seat of the beast or the headquarters of the beast, and his kingdom was plunged into darkness. The beast here represents primarily the papacy in its revived state, not only in religious matters, but as a world power. This is the same beast we saw in Revelation 13:1-5 and Satan gave him power, his seat, and great authority. The plagues moved from a lesser intensity to a greater intensity. The angels started with the sores, then a terrible odor in the world, then they moved on to a lack of drinking water, then darkness and confusion among the leaders of the world. The sixth angel poured out his bowl on the great river Euphrates and her many canals and immediately the water dried up so that the way of the king of the east might be prepared. The sixth angel added another aspect to the equation. A spiritual and a physical war. Sores, odor, no water, and terrible heat everywhere, darkness and confusion among the leaders of the world, and now war

Travelling Through Rough Waters

had broken out over the entire globe.

The seventh angel poured out his bowl into the earth's atmosphere, and all across the sky were flashes of lighting, followed by thunder and an earthquake so severe that the entire planet shook. Entire islands disappeared, and large mountains simply dropped out of sight. The earthquake was followed by a global hailstorm, with each hailstone weighing about one hundred pounds. When the plagues were over, the earth looked like a wilderness. Many strongly believe that mankind will finally destroy itself someday on planet earth with nuclear weapons. It is true that mankind will do damage to the earth, but the Bible predicts the ultimate destruction of the earth before God creates a new heaven and a new earth, and this ultimate destruction is found in the seven last plagues.

One group of people that will not need to worry about the destruction of this world, are those people who truly love God and their fellow men and keep God's commandments and the testimony of Jesus. The Bible says,

He who comes to the secret place of the Most High will find rest in the shadow of the Almighty. I will say of the Lord, "He is my refuge and fortress, my God, the One I can trust." He will deliver you from Satan's trap and from the deadly disease of sin. He will cover you with His feathers and hide you under His wings. His truth will defend and protect you. Don't be afraid of the enemy who attacks at night, nor of his arrows that fly by day. Don't be afraid of sickness that spreads at night, nor of the plague that strikes during the day. A thousand may

The Seven Last Plagues

fall beside you and ten thousand die around you, but if the Lord decrees, death will not come near you. With your own eyes you will see what happens to the wicked. This is because you have made the Lord your defender and the Most High your refuge. (Ps. 91)

The prophetess Ellen G. White gives us a synoptic view of the condition during the seven last plagues. This is what she says, "Many of the wicked were enraged as they suffered the effects of the plagues. It was a scene of fearful agony. Parents were bitterly reproaching their children, and children their parents, brothers their sisters, and sisters their brothers. Loud wailing cries were heard in every direction. "It was you who kept me from receiving the truth which would have saved me from this awful hour." The people turned upon their ministers with bitter hate and reproached them, saying, "You have not warned us. You told us that all the world was to be converted, and cried, Peace, peace, to quiet every fear that was aroused. You have not told us of this hour, and those who warned us of this hour you declared them to be fanatics and evil men who would ruin us. But I saw that the Ministers did not escape the wrath of God. Their suffering was tenfold greater than that of their people." *(Early Writings, 282)*

Here's what she says about the saints who will be living during the seven last plagues: Angels provided them food and water, while the wicked were suffering from hunger and thirst. I saw the leading men of the earth consulting together, and Satan and his angels busy around them. I saw a writing, copies of which were scattered in different parts of the land, giving orders that unless the saints

Travelling Through Rough Waters

should yield their peculiar faith, give up the Sabbath, and observe the first day of the week, the people were at liberty after a certain time to put them to death....In some places, before the time for the decree to be executed, the wicked rushed upon the saints to slay them, but angels in the form of men of war fought for them....

Satan wished to have the privilege of destroying the saints of the Most High, but Jesus bade His angels watch over them. God would be honored by making a covenant with those who had kept His law, in the sight of the heathen round about them. Jesus would be honored by translating them without their seeing death.... Next came the multitude of the angry wicked, and next a mass of evil angels, hurrying on the wicked to slay the saints, but before they could approach God's people, the wicked must first pass this company of mighty holy angels. This was impossible. The angels of God were causing them to recede and also causing the evil angels who were pressing around them to fall back. (*Early Writings*, 282-283)

I am moved by the message of the seven last plagues. It is my desire that all who read this chapter of the book think very seriously about it and seek God's guidance in this matter. If you are a Bible-believing Christian, you must agree with me that this subject will affect everyone who is living on planet earth in the near future.

Chapter 6

Traveling on Rough Waters

Acts, chapter 27, tells us a story about a storm. It could be considered a tropical cyclone. This experience took place a long time ago. Paul, an apostle of Christ, was in this storm, and he gave the summary of what happen. He said he was on a voyage to Rome and his ship ran into a storm. The storm was threatening. He said, "We sailed for many days without seeing the sun or the moon and stars." The storm struck the ship so hard

Travelling Through Rough Waters

that it was almost impossible for the captain to keep it on course. Soon they gave up and let the ship be carried by the wind. They decided to drop anchor and have everyone vacate the ship and try to make it on their own. Paul stood to his feet in the ship and told them, "Except ye abide in the ship ye shall not be saved."

I like the way the King James Version interprets Acts 27:27. The KJV called the storm "Euroclydon," which means "Rough Waters." There was no doubt that the ship was experiencing rough waters. The church of God is described by many as the "Old Ship of Zion." The Old Ship of Zion is captained by King Jesus. This ship has been struck many times by forces equal or even stronger than Euroclydon, but she is still sailing along. The Christian journey is often described as a ship sailing on high seas, and the boisterous wind attacks our ship from every side. We will look at how each of these attacks from Euroclydon upon the Old Ship of Zion affect the passengers on board. Satan's attack on God's church can be seen like the forces of Euroclydon. I would like to look at a few of these attacks on the Old Ship of Zion, and I will call each attack "Euroclydon."

First Attack on the Old Ship of Zion

Euroclydon's first attacked the Old Ship of Zion when she left the harbor with our first parents, and the ship took a nosedive that led to the destruction of millions of people on the face of the earth. It was Satan's plan to take over the captain of the ship. He was so sure of himself, that one day he went to heaven boasting of his skills and expertise in taking over the ship. This is how the prophet described the conversation with him and God in the Book of Job, "In heaven, representatives from various planets in God's created universe come together regularly to meet with Him. One day Satan also came and presented himself for admittance. God said to him, 'On what basis do you want to attend this meeting?' and Satan answered and said, 'I am from planet earth where I have been roaming back and forth for a long time'" (Job 1:6-1-10, *Clear Word Bible*).

In this statement, "roaming back and forth," Lucifer is pointing out to God that the only reason he can roam freely in the earth, is because it belongs to him. But God asked him a question that he was unable to answer, "What about my servant Job?" Euroclydon has struck the Old Ship of Zion, but she is still sailing.

Euroclydon's Second Attack on the Old Ship of Zion

The Old Ship of Zion took another hit from Euroclydon when some of the passengers on board decided to abandon ship and formed the bedrock of idolatry and paganism. Genesis 11:1-9 tells us,

At first all the descendants of Noah had only one language. As they moved east from Mount Ararat where the ark had settled, they made their homes in the plain of Shinar, also called Mesopotamia. After some time they said to each other, "Come, let's build permanent places to live. We'll use baked bricks and tar instead of sandstone and mortar." When this was successful, they said, "Now that we've built this beautiful city, let's erect a huge escape tower to protect ourselves against any

Travelling Through Rough Waters

future flood. People from other cities will come to see and we will become famous. Then the Lord came down to take a look at the city and the escape tower they were building, and said, "This is only the beginning of what these people will attempt to do. They all speak the same language, and if they succeed in this, they'll think that they can do anything they set their mind to. We need to stop them so they don't become proud and forget who created them. Let's confuse their language so they can't communicate so easily with each other." And that's what happened. Soddenly the people start speaking different languages and could not understand each other. Building on the tower and the city stopped, and people move away. The area became known as Babylon or Babel, which means "confusion," because that was where the Lord confounded the language of the people. (*Clear Word Bible*)

Nimrod, the great-grandson of Noah, was the leading figure in walking away from the family religious practice. He rebelled against God and formed the bedrock of paganism. Nimrod built Babylon, Assyria, and Nineveh and he became the first sun god. Every form of witchcraft and pagan practice today has some link to Nimrod. The arch-deceiver found a man whom he could use to strike terror to the Old Ship of Zion, but the ship is still sailing.

The Babel builders had indulged the spirit of murmuring against God. Instead of gratefully remembering His mercy to Adam and His gracious covenant with Noah, they had complained of His severity in expelling the first parent from Eden and destroying the world by a flood. But while they murmured against God as arbitrary and severe, they were accepting the rule of the cruelest of tyrants. Satan was seeking to bring contempt upon the sacrificial offerings that prefigured the death of Christ; and as the minds of the people were darkened by idolatry, he led them to counterfeit these offerings and sacrifice their own children upon the altars of their gods. As men turned away from God, the divine attributes—justice, purity, and love—were supplanted by oppression, violence, and brutality. For a time the descendants of Noah continued to dwell among the mountains where the ark had rested. As their numbers increased, apostasy soon led to division.

Those who desired to forget their Creator and to cast off the restraint of His law felt a constant annoyance from the teaching and example of their God-fearing associates, and after a time they decided to separate from the worshipers of God. Accordingly they journeyed to the plain of Shinar, on the banks of the river Euphrates. They were attracted by the beauty of the land and the fertility of the soil, and upon this plain they determined to make their home. (*Patriarchs and Prophets*, Ch. 9 "The Tower of Babel")

Euroclydon's Third Attack on the Old Ship of Zion

The Old Ship of Zion was hit by Euroclydon a third time when she was held captive in Egypt for 450 years and it was only by the flexing of the Almighty's muscles that she was led out of captivity. We read in Exodus 1:8-16:

Then a foreign king began to rule over Egypt who didn't want to know about Joseph and what he had done to save Egypt (Joseph was a Hebrew who interpreted

Travelling Through Rough Waters

the king's dream and because of his interpretation of the king's dream the people of Egypt were saved from starvation). According to this new king, In case of war, they might join the enemy and fight us, or they might leave the country, which would greatly jeopardize our economy. We need them, but we must stop them from having so many children.

So the Egyptians sent troops into the land of Goshen and set slave masters over the children of Israel to crush their spirits with hard labor, forcing them to build cities like Pithom and Rameses which became supply centers for Pharaoh. But the harder they were forced to work, the more they multiplied, and the more land they needed to live on. Soon the Egyptians became afraid of them. They tried to protect themselves by making their Israelite slaves work even harder. They made life extremely difficult for the Israelites by ruthlessly forcing them to work on the king's building projects and in his fields in the bitterly hot sun. One day Pharaoh called in Shiphrah and Puah, the Hebrew midwives in charge of those who delivered babies, and said to them, When you and your assistants help a Hebrew woman deliver her baby, if it's a boy, kill him, but if it's a girl let her live. That's an order. (*The Clear Word Bible*)

Satan himself was the main instigator encouraging the king and council to take this drastic measure against the children of Israel. He is always after God's interest on planet earth. Ellen G. White state in Patriarchs and prophets that

orders were issued to the women to destroy the Hebrew male children at their birth. Satan was the mover in this matter. He knew that a deliverer was to be raised up among the Israelites; and by leading the king to destroy their children he hoped to defeat the divine purpose. But the women feared God, and dared not execute the cruel mandate. The Lord approved their course, and prospered them. The king, angry at the failure of his design, made the command more urgent and extensive. The whole nation was called upon to hunt out and slaughter his helpless victims. And Pharaoh charged all his people, saying, "Every son that is born ye shall cast into the river, and every daughter ye shall save alive." (*Patriarchs and Prophets*, Ch. 21 "Moses")

God moved in and delivered the Old Ship of Zion. He designed a way to spare the life of Moses, who became the deliverer of God's people. The ship was damaged, but she is still sailing along.

Euroclydon's Fourth Attack on the Old Ship of Zion

The Old Ship of Zion was hit by Euroclydon the fourth time when Haman tried to rid the earth of the only people that preserved the knowledge of the true God. Esther 3:10-15 tells us,

The king listened to Haman and was pleased with what he heard. So he took off the ring which he used to stamp his seal on royal proclamations and loaned it to Haman, son of Hammedatha and descendant of Agag, king of the Amalekites who had been bitter enemies of the Jews. The king said to Haman, "Write out the execution order, seal it with my ring, and when you've confiscated their property, all their silver will be yours to manage

Travelling Through Rough Waters

for the good of the country." So on the thirteenth day of the first month, Haman called in the royal secretaries and dictated an order to be translated into every language used in the empire and sent to all the nobles, governors and officials throughout the land. The order was written in the name of the king and sealed with his ring. Then Haman returned the ring to the king. Royal couriers took the king's order to all parts of the empire that on the thirteenth day of the month of Adar, the last month in the year, all Jews, young and old, men, women and children, were to be killed for their disloyalty, completely annihilated in one day.

Their property was to be confiscated and sold and the money put into the royal treasury. The order was to be read publicly and then posted so the people would be ready to carry out the king's order when the day came. The decree was first issued in the capital city of Susa; then the couriers were sent to every province in the empire. The king and Haman sat down and toasted each other, but the people in the city were stunned and confused by the king's irrational behavior. (Clear Word Bible)

It should be noted that this situation happened in the Medo-Persian kingdom, the second world power. Haman intended to kill every Jew who was living on the face of the earth. The letters were sent from India to Ethiopia, 127 provinces in all, to every province in its own script, to every people in their own language, and to the Jews in their own script and language. Haman's idea was diabolical. This is what the prophets said about Naman's plans, "Misled by the false statements of Haman, Xerxes was induced to issue a decree providing for the massacre of all the Jews scattered abroad and dispersed among the people in all the provinces of the Medo-Persian kingdom. Little did the king realized the far-reaching results that would have accompanied the complete carrying out of this decree. Satan himself, the hidden instigator of the scheme, was trying to rid the earth of those who preserved the knowledge of the true God." (Ellen G. White, Prophets and Kings 600-601)

The Old Ship of Zion Was Hit the Fifth Time by Euroclydon

The Old Ship of Zion was hit the fifth time by Euroclydon when some of the passengers on board put the captain of the ship to death, but even then, the ship kept moving along, because the gates of hell shall not prevail against this ship. When Lucifer realized that using the people from outside of the ship did not work, he decided to make friends with the passengers on board. Isaiah prophesied thousands of years before, that the Messiah would come and liberate His people; however, when the Messiah came, Lucifer inspired the people to reject Him. This is what Isaiah said, "For unto us a Child will be born, to us a Son will be given, and the government will rest on His shoulders. He will be called The Wonderful Counselor, The Mighty God, The Everlasting Father, The Prince of Peace. Of the increase of His government there will be no end. He will sit on David's throne and rule the kingdom. He will do what is right and just from the time He takes the throne and forever. The great God of heaven and earth, the Lord Almighty Himself, will do this." (Isaiah 9:6-7).

Travelling Through Rough Waters

The Angel Spoke to Joseph
One night Joseph was putting together his wedding plans to marry Mary. As he was considering how to carry out his plans, an angel appeared to him in a dream and said, "Joseph, don't be concerned about Mary's purity (the angel said this to Joseph because Mary got pregnant and she told Joseph that she didn't know how it happened because she had not have sexual intercourse with anyone). Go ahead and marry her. She's still a virgin, in spite of what you think. She was made pregnant through the power of the Holy Spirit and will give birth to the Messiah. When the baby is born, I want you to name Him Jesus, because He will save His people from their Sins" All this happened just as it had been predicted centuries ago by the prophet Isaiah: "A young woman who is still a virgin will conceive and give birth to a Son. He will be called Emmanuel, meaning God Is with Us." When Joseph woke up, he followed the angel's instruction and married Mary, but decided not to have sexual relations with her until after God's Son was born. Joseph named Him Jesus as the angel had instructed him." (Matt. 1:20-25, *Clear Word Bible*)

The Angel Spoke to Mary
Your pregnancy will be by the power of the Holy Spirit, and the Baby you give birth to will be holy because you'll be giving birth to the Son of God. (Luke 1:35, *Clear Word Bible*)

The Angel Spoke to the Shepherds
Suddenly the angel Gabriel appeared to them, and God's glory surrounded them. The shepherds were terrified.

Traveling on Rough Waters

But he said to them, "Don't be afraid. I'm bringing you good news that will thrill your hearts and bring joy to people everywhere. A few hours ago, the Lord's Messiah, your Savior, was born in Bethlehem, the city of David. This is how you will know Him: You'll find Him lying in a manger, wrapped in strips of cloth. (Luke 2:9-12, *Clear Word Bible*)

I pointed out these clear scriptural evidences about the Messiah because it was impossible for anyone to miss these clear evidences about the Messiah, but Lucifer got into the ship with the passengers and by the time he got done with them, all the leaders missed the reason for their spiritual journey. Not only did they miss the most important phase of their journey, but they became very aggressive toward the Messiah and the atmosphere was diabolical. Just listen to what took place at Pilate's Judgment Hall:

Then he [Pilate] called for Jesus, who was brought out wearing the crown of thorns and the purple robe. Pilate said, "Look at the Man! He's covered with blood! What more do you want?" When the chief priests and temple officers saw Jesus, they said, "We want Him crucified!" Then the mob started shouting, "Crucify Him! Crucify Him!" The Jewish leaders said, "According to our law, He ought to die because He claims to be the Son of God." When Pilate heard that, he was afraid, so he took Jesus back inside and said to Him, "Where did you originally come from?" Jesus stood without answering. Pilate looked at Jesus and said, "Aren't you going to answer me? Don't you know that I have The power to have you crucified or to let you go?" Jesus answered, "Actually,

Travelling Through Rough Waters

you couldn't do a thing to me unless heaven allowed it. But those who brought me to you will have the greater guilt."

After this, Pilate tried even harder to release Jesus, but the Jewish leaders kept reminding him that such an act would put him in opposition to Caesar by letting someone go who claimed to be the King of Judea. Pilate immediately sensed the seriousness of the situation. He knew that the Jews would not hesitate to accuse him of protecting a rival king before the emperor. The mob shouted back, "Take Him away! Crucify Him!" Pilate cried out again, "You mean I should crucify your King?" The crowd, encouraged by the Jewish leaders, shouted louder than ever, "We have no king but Caesar!" Then Pilate pronounced the sentence and turned Jesus over to the soldiers for crucifixion. And they led Him away. They took Jesus to the courtyard below and placed on His shoulders the heavy crossbeam to carry to a place outside the city called Golgotha, meaning The Place of the Skull. There they crucified Jesus between two of Barabbas's men, one on His right and the other on His left. (Luke 19:5-18, *Clear Word Bible*)

For a time the Old Ship of Zion was on autopilot, but the Old Ship of Zion is high-tech. The Holy Spirit locked the ship into cruise control while the pilot was sleeping. They crucified the Messiah on Friday and put Him into a borrowed tomb, but early Sunday morning an angel shot down the Milky Way galaxy with speed faster than light. Ellen G. White tells us that this angel is the same angel who fills the position from which Satan fell. This was the same angel who proclaimed Christ's birth. This angel was so mighty that even the Demons fled from the tomb where Christ was buried. When his feet touched down on planet earth, there was a mighty earthquake, the earth tossed about like a drunken man, and he told Jesus, "They Father calleth Thee." (Mark 16:1-7, *The Desire of Ages*, 779-782).

Jesus got up and left two angels at the burial ground to informed the passengers on board, as to the whereabouts of the Captain while He went to His Father for an approval of His sacrifice.

The Old Ship of Zion Was Hit the Sixth Time by Euroclydon

The Old ship of Zion received a major blow by Euroclydon through the wicked and persecuting hand of Nero, who was the fifth emperor of Rome. After the Captain of the ship arose and ascended to heaven, Lucifer was furious. He decided to attack the passengers on board, so he started a persecution, beginning with Nero and continuing for centuries. Christians were falsely accused of the most dreadful crimes and declared to be the cause of great calamities, famines, pestilences, and earthquakes. They were condemned as rebels against the empire, as foes of religion, and pests to society. Great numbers were thrown to wild beasts or burned alive in the amphitheaters. Some were crucified; others were covered with the skins of wild animals and thrust into the arena to be torn by dogs. Their punishment was often made the chief entertainment at public fairs. Vast multitudes assembled to enjoy the sight and greeted their dying agonies with laughter and applause. Beneath the hills outside the city

Travelling Through Rough Waters

of Rome, long galleries had been tunneled through the earth. Dark passageways extended for miles beyond the city wall. In these underground caverns, the followers of Christ lived and buried their dead. When Christ shall descend from heaven the second time to gather His people, many of them will come forth from those gloomy caverns (Ellen G. White, *The Great Controversy* p.40).

Paul, writing to the members of the church, alluded to this persecution:

Do you recall when God's truth and light first penetrated your heart? Remember how willing you were to suffer for Him and you didn't let your troubles and problems crush your faith? Remember how you were put on public display and were laughed at, insulted and handled roughly? Do you recall how eager you were to defend your faith in Christ and how willing you were to fellowship with those who were being persecuted for it? You had compassion on those who were arrested and put in prison and you suffered along with them. You even took it joyfully when they broke into your houses and took your belongings because you knew that you had better and lasing possession in heaven. (Hebrews 10:32-34, *Clear Word Bible*)

Many were cruelly mocked and whipped, put in chains and imprisoned. Others have been stoned to death, sawed in half, killed by the sword. Others wore sheepskins or goatskins, they were poor, persecuted and mistreated. For them the comforts of this world were not worth losing faith in God. They became refugees and wandered in deserts and mountains, making their homes in caves and holes in the ground. (Hebrews 11:36-38, *Clear Word Bible*)

The Old Ship of Zion Was Hit the Seventh Time by Euroclydon

The seventh and most diabolical attack by Euroclydon was Satan's scheme to compromise with the persecuted saints. The persecution by Satan did not deter the passengers on board. Millions of saints were martyrs, but their blood became spiritual fertilizer for the seeds of the gospel. Thousands were imprisoned and slain, but others sprang up and fill their places. Their suffering brought Christians nearer to each other and to their Redeemer. When Satan realized that his efforts were not accomplishing the result he intended, he changed his strategy. He laid his plans to war more successfully against the government of God by planting his banner in the Christian church.

In his mind, he calculated that if the followers of Christ could be deceived and led to displease God, then their strength, fortitude, and firmness would fail, and they would fall as easy prey. This is not the first time we see Satan doing this same trick on the church of God. Come with me and I will show you what he did before. Balak, the king of Moab, was very much afraid of the Israelites when they were on their way to the promised land, so he called Balaam, a so-called prophet who lived in Mesopotamia, and asked him to come and put a curse on the Israelites. Balaam went and tried to put the curse on the people, but he could not. When he realized that he could not curse the people, Satan told him to trick

Travelling Through Rough Waters

the people of God. This is what he did: Balaam suggested that Balak should have a grand festival to honor their gods and it was secretly arranged that Balaam should induce the Israelites to attend. Balaam was regarded by the Israelites as a prophet of God; therefore, it was not difficult for him to accomplish his purpose. Great numbers of the people joined him in witnessing the festivities. They ventured upon forbidden ground and were entangled in the snare of Satan.

Beguiled with music and dancing, and allured by the beauty of heathen women, they cast off their oath or pledge of allegiance to God. As they united in mirth and feasting, indulgence in wine, their mind and their senses became beclouded and the barriers of self-control were broken down. Having defiled their consciences, they were persuaded to bow down to idols. They offered sacrifice upon the heathen altar and participated in the most degrading rites. Their iniquitous practices did to Israel what all the enchantments of Balaam could not do, they separated themselves from God. (*Patriarchs and Prophets*, 454-455)

In the seventh great attack from Euroclydon we notice that Satan is about to duplicate the same trick he did with the Israelites at Mount Peor. After he realized that his plan to persecute the saints was not accomplishing what he had wanted, he decided to trick them. Persecution ceased and instead there was temporal prosperity and worldly honor. The state became a friend of Christianity. There was a compromise with the pure doctrine of Christianity. Idolatry was received as part of the Christian faith, while they rejected other essential truths. They professed to accept Jesus as the Son of God and to believe in His death and resurrection, but they had no conviction of sin and felt no need for repentance or a change of heart.

The church was in fearful peril. Prison, torture, fire, and sword were a blessing in comparison to this. Some of the Christians stood firm, declaring that they would not compromise; but others were in favor of yielding or modifying some features of their faith and uniting with those who had accepted a part of Christianity, urging that this might be the means of the heathens full conversion. Under the cloak of false Christianity, Satan was subtly manipulating and maneuvering himself into the church to corrupt their faith and turn the minds of the people from the Word of God. Most of the Christians at last consented to lower their standard and a union was formed between Christianity and paganism. Paganism, however, still clung to their idolatry, only changing the object of their worship to the image of Jesus, Mary, and the saints. Unsound doctrine, superstitious rites, and idolatrous ceremonies were incorporated into the faith and worship (*The Great Controversy*, 42-43).

The papacy today is the result of this union of paganism and Christianity. Paul, in his letter to the Thessalonians, alluded to this powerful system:

Let no one deceive you by any means, for that day will not come unless the falling away comes first, and the man of sin is revealed, who opposes and exalts himself above all that is called God or that is worship, so that he sits as God in the temple of God, showing himself that he is God. Do you remember that when I was still with

Travelling Through Rough Waters

you I told you these things? And now you know what is restraining him, so that he may be revealed in his own time. (2 Thess. 2:3-7)

Little by little and then more openly as this system increased in strength and gained control of the minds of man, the mystery of iniquity carried forward its deceptive and blasphemous work. The customs of heathenism found their way into the Christian church. The spirit of compromise and conformity was restrained for a time, but as persecution ceased and Christianity entered the courts and palaces of kings, she laid aside the humble simplicity of Christ for the pomp and pride of pagan priests and rulers. The world cloaked with a form of righteousness walked into the church.

This compromise between paganism and Christianity resulted in the development of the "Man of sin" that was prophesied by the Apostle Paul. This man of sin is this gigantic religious system, the masterpiece of Satan's power that is opposing and exalting himself above God. Satan endeavored to form a similar compromise with Jesus. He went to Jesus in the wilderness and showed Jesus all the kingdoms of the world and offered to give them to Christ if He would but acknowledge his supremacy as the prince of darkness. Christ rebuked him and forced him to depart from Him. He was not successful with Christ, but when he made the same offer to the Christian church he was meet with greater success.

To secure worldly gains and honors, the church was led to seek the favor and support of the great men of earth, and having thus rejected Christ, she was induced to yield allegiance to the representative of Satan—the bishop of Rome. It is one of the leading doctrines of Romanism that the pope is the visible head of the universal church of Christ, invested with supreme authority over bishops and pastors in all parts of the world. The pope has been given the very titles of Deity and has been declared infallible. He demanded the homage of all mankind, the same claim urged by Satan in the wilderness and is still urged by him through the Church of Rome today, and vast numbers are ready to yield him homage.

God has never given even a hint in His word that He has appointed any man to be head of His church. Satan or the pope can have no power over Christ's church except by usurpation. In order for Satan to maintain his sway over men, and establish the authority of the papal usurper, he must keep them in ignorance of the scriptures. Satan knew that the Bible would exalt God and place finite man in his true position; therefore, the sacred truths were concealed and suppressed. This idea was adopted by the Roman Church for hundreds of years, and the circulation of the Bible was prohibited (*The Great Controversy*, 50-51).

The Future of the Old Ship of Zion

According to Revelation, Euroclydon is not finished; he has some future attack for the Old Ship of Zion. This is what John the Revelator said:

Then I was given another vision. I saw a huge beast which looked like nothing I had ever seen before come up out of the sea. In a way, it was similar to the dragon because it also had seven heads and ten horns, but this beast had ten crowns instead of seven, one on each

Travelling Through Rough Waters

horn. Blasphemous words against God were written on each head.

This sea beast had the body of a leopard, the paws of a bear, and each head had the mouth of a lion. The dragon gave this beast its power, its earthly throne and great spiritual authority. The dragon used this beast to deceive and kill God's people. I saw one of the heads of this sea beast suddenly go limp as if it had been fatally wounded. This greatly affected the beast and it looked as if it would bleed to death, but suddenly the wound was healed and it was well again. Then I saw the beast begin to walk the earth. Everywhere it went, people were influenced by its charm. Soon they were worshiping this beast and said to each other, "Who is as powerful as this huge beast, and who would dare fight against it?"

But they didn't realize that by worshiping the beast, they were worshiping the dragon that had given the beast its power and spirit. This beast made all sorts of religious claims for itself and even blasphemed God by claiming to speak for God....It continued to blaspheme God and those who dwell in heaven by misusing His name and undermining the truth of His dwelling place in heaven. Then the dragon gave power to the beast to make war against God's people to overcome them. Soon it exercised its authority over every tribe, people, language and nation. Everyone on earth worships the sea beast all those whose names had not been written in the Book of life belonging to the Lamb of God who was willing to die for us before this world was created. He who has ears should listen to what I'm saying. (Rev. 13:1-9, *Clear Word Bible*)

A couple things you should know to understand the above passage or the future activity of Satan's attack upon the Old Ship of Zion or God's church. First of all, a beast in biblical prophecy represents the power or kingdom (Dan. 7:17, 23). So the beast John saw in his vision is not a natural beast, but a certain power on the earth with a person leading the organization. Remember, Satan has to use people in his affairs with mankind, because he is not permitted to be visibly involved in man's affairs.) Water in biblical prophecy represents people or masses of people (Rev. 17:15). So the water that John saw is not natural water; it is masses of people, or the more densely populated areas of the world. The crown in biblical prophecy represents rulers or kingdoms (Ezek. 21:26-27). The crowns John saw in his vision are not literal crowns, but rulers or kingdoms. The Dragon in biblical prophecy represents the Devil or Satan (Rev. 12:7-9).

Let us try to understand what John the Revelator is saying. According to John, the future attack on the Old Ship of Zion, or the church of God, will come from a powerful religious system on the earth in the last days, and this powerful religious system will receive its power from the Devil. This religious system will be a worldwide religious system. You can tell that it is a religious system based on the text. John said, "Everyone on the earth whose name that is not written in the book of life will worship the beast [or will worship a man who has received his power from the Dragon or Lucifer] (Rev. 13:8). It should be noted that as the people worshiped this beast they were also worshiping the Devil, because it was the Devil who gave his power to this

Travelling Through Rough Waters

beast that made him so powerful (Rev. 13:2,4).

Please note that I use the names Lucifer, Satan, Dragon, and the Devil interchangeably because all of these names refer to the same person or spirit (Rev. 12:9). What I notice is that Lucifer's final attack on the Old Ship of Zion is the final phase of a fight started in heaven long ago, and the final score is about to be settled on the earth (Rev. 12:7). The fight started in heaven with Lucifer and God. Then Lucifer dragged the angels into it, and now he is dragging the human family into it to settle the score of this age-old fight. This fight is not good for the human family, because those who took sides with Lucifer will be going to hell with him. Then something happened to the angels in heaven; those who took sides with Lucifer were thrown out of heaven and are now waiting for hellfire (Rev. 12:9).

I notice something in this prophetic vision that John had. The Dragon, or Lucifer, is using the beast (Rev. 13:2). This beast is represented by a man leading this religious system on planet earth. This position is usual for human beings. People do not aspire for the position of the great God of the universe except when they are inspired by an antagonistic spirit or influence. The idea that this beast—this man claiming to be God or claiming to speak for God—is diabolical (Rev. 13:4-5). Claiming worship, which belongs only to God, is a very serious thing. Not even the angels from heaven allow such thought to go through their minds. There was a time in John's ministry when an angel was sent to him to give him instruction, and John was so terrified that he fell on his knees before the angel. The angel immediately reached forth and

Traveling on Rough Waters

picked John from off his knees and told him, "Don't kneel in front of me. I am just a servant of God like you are.... God is the One to worship" (Rev. 19:10, 22:8-9, *Clear Word Bible*).

Who is this man or religious system Lucifer is using on the earth today? Let us try to find out in the chapter titled "The Mark of the Beast." So, we find Lucifer making his final attack on the Old Ship of Zion and this attack is even more devastating than any of the previous attacks. This time he comes in full force and anyone who lives on earth, who refuses to obey his command, Satan's plan is to kill him/her (Rev. 13:7). But the Captain of the Old Ship of Zion, the One who was dead, the One whose resurrection caused a mighty earthquake on planet earth, the One who was dead but could have raised up Himself if He wanted to, tells us in 1 Thessalonians 4:13 that he is about to take the ship into harbor. He will be dropping anchor in a little while. The final furlong will be bloody, but nothing in the universe will stop the Old Ship of Zion from reaching its final destination. Satan, your hands are too short to box with the Lord. You may not go down in the first round. You may not go down in the second and third rounds. You might even last until the tenth round, but you are going down because the gates of hell shall not prevail against the Captain of the Old Ship of Zion.

Chapter 7

The Great Gulf Fixed

The Jews used to have many folktales that they used to teach moral lessons. Jesus used one of their folktales in Luke 16. In telling this story Jesus intended to teach us that our future destiny is determined by the use we make of the opportunities of this present life. There is no after probation for anyone when he or she dies. If one dies without making things right with the Lord, there will be a fixed and impassable gulf between him and God. According to the story, there were two church members; one was rich and the other was poor.

The Great Gulf Fixed

Jesus said the poor brother was full of sores, and running bumps. He was so weak that he could not drive the flies and the dogs away as they licked his sores. This beggar sat at the rich man's gate, desiring to be fed with the very crumbs that fell from the table. He was not bothering the rich man, but it was obvious that he needed some food.

The rich man, on the other hand, did not openly show his disregard for his brother, the beggar; he just ignored him, acted as if he was not there. The process went on for a long time. Jesus said the poor man, or the beggar, finally died and was carried to Abraham's bosom. It was typically known among the Jews that when one talks about Abraham's Bosom, he is speaking of a place call paradise. Abraham's Lap is a place where the blessed dead will one day go (speaking of the first resurrection). The one who dies in the Lord will wind up some day in Abraham's Lap. Abraham's Bosom and Abraham's Lap mean the same thing.

Then after a while the other brother died and went to hell. While he was in hell he looked and saw his poor brother in Abraham's lap, so he called out to Abraham and told him to send his brother to him with some water, because it was very hot down there in hell. Abraham told the rich brother that he could not do that, because when he was alive he had everything and his brother had nothing, not to mention there was a great gulf fixed and no one can come from me to you and no one can come from you to me. This rich man represents every man and woman who makes a wrong use of life's opportunities. The beggar was a Christian (he was a Sabbath keeper).

Travelling Through Rough Waters

We understand this fact because he was associated with Abraham. All who truly become a part of Abraham's descendants, whether by birth or spiritually engrafted, are commandment keepers. It should be noted that, according to the original, all who associated with Father Abraham kept God's commandments.

The rich man was also a so-called child of God. We know this to be true, because he called Abraham father, and all of Abraham's children were supposed to be religious. Abraham was the father of the faithful, so when a person called Abraham father, he was declaring that he, too, adhered to Abraham's faith and beliefs. The rich man also died, but he went to another place called hell. This shows us that many people in the church will not be saved in God's kingdom. They are in God's church, but they are dancing to the beat of a different drum. Luke 16:24 sends a chill down your spine as you see what is going on in the verse because it comes home to us. The rich man also called Abraham father, which gives us the right to see him as a member of the same church that the beggar attends. He was a brother who treated his brother like a dog. Verse 25 verifies the fact that the rich man was a member of the same church that the beggar attended. In verse 25 Abraham did not deny the fact that the rich man was one of his children, because he himself called him son. Many Christians sing in church this song, "Father Abraham had many sons, many sons had father Abraham. I am one of them and so are you, so just let's praise the Lord."

Because we are a part of the same family, we need to be loving and kind to each other. We need to look

The Great Gulf Fixed

out for each other. The Bible says, "How good it is for brothers and sisters to dwell together in love and unity," (Ps. 133:1). This is where the message comes home to us. Here are two men; both of them called themselves Abraham's child, which gives us the legitimate right to see both of them as members of God's church. They sat together in church every week, prayed together, sang together, and washed each other feet during communion service. You could not tell that both were not true Christians who looked forward to the second coming of our Lord and Savior Jesus Christ. But one of these men missed heaven because he did not care about his brother.

It is not a light thing to act like you don't care about people around you who need help, and more so, people who are of the same household of faith. According to Luke, both men died in the church. Both received a dignified funeral service by the pastor of the church; but while the eulogy was being performed, the angel was writing down one of the men's name in the Book of Life and the other's name in the Book of Death. Sad commentary, but that's the way it will be for many of us when we die if we are not careful. One of the members struggles with the realities of life and decides not to surrender, the other member struggles with the realities of life and decides to surrender all to Jesus.

Some may say it is understandable that Lazarus, the poor man, would be the one to surrender because he had nothing, but you and I have seen that poverty, shame, and disgrace have driven many from the Lord. The poor man could have complained about his situation. He could

Travelling Through Rough Waters

have dwelled on the fact that God was not fair, because He had silver and gold and cattle upon a thousand hills; however, He allowed his faithful child to suffer hunger and thirst and die a shameful death.

But, he allowed no such accusation to come from his mouth. He accepted his lot in life and looked forward to a land that is fairer than day, and by faith he could see it afar because his Father waits over the way to prepare him a dwelling place there. In the sweet by and by, he sang, I shall meet with God on that beautiful shore. Sometimes life seems unfair and it is very easy for some people to get mad with God because of their situation in life.

There are many people in the church who suffer many things. They are faithful and they are trying to do their best, but it seems as if the harder they try the worse things get. They try to reason with God, and it seems as if they are cut off from Him, but if you will allow me to make a suggestion, I suggest that you hold on, better days are coming, don't let go, Jesus is watching over you. If you are faithful, He will see you through. In Luke 16: 30, the rich man who went to hell blamed God and the prophets indirectly for not giving him enough warning. No one drives home to me the seriousness of doing the right thing. No one drives home to my mind the important of fixing my heart on Christ regardless of my situation.

According to the story, Abraham cut him off at the path and told him, "you had Moses and the prophets" You had the Word of God. In the Judgment men will reason that they did not get enough information in regards

The Great Gulf Fixed

to their salvation and their duty to their fellow men, but God will make it very clear that all men have a fair chance to make it into the kingdom. Today, I thank God for those men and women across the globe who are serving God. You might run into some rocky mountain, you might have to climb up the rough side of the mountain, you might find yourselves crying in the middle of the night, but Jesus will be the captain of your ship and He will take you to the promised land. Stay in God's church even if it kills you. Do not go anywhere and the great God of heaven will see you through.

There is a great gulf fixed so no one can come from me to you and from you to me. In other words, there is no communication between the living and the dead. Everything should be fixed before you and I depart from this world. The word gulf here represents the difference in moral character between the rich man and the poor man. There is a big difference between Lazarus's Christlike character and the rich man's character. Our character makes the difference. Many of us look just alike. We go to church every week and participate in church activities, but our characters are far from pure. This one aspect of our being makes the difference in where we spend our eternity.

Abraham told the rich man that there is a great gulf fixed. The word fixed makes reference to the fact that after death our character cannot be change. It is fixed forever. So if you go down like a brute you will raised up like a brute. If you go down an ungodly person you will be raised up as an ungodly person. If you go down as a righteous person you will be raised up as a righteous

Travelling Through Rough Waters

person. If you and I go down with a Christ-like character, on that great getting-up morning we will get up in the first resurrection and cry out, "O Grave, where is thy victory, O death, where is thy sting." After a man or a woman dies it is over for him or her, so today if you hear my voice, Jesus said harden not your heart, because tomorrow you may die, and it may be too late.

Chapter 8

The People of the Kingdom

In Mark, chapter 4, Jesus described the different groups of people in the church. He described hearts as soil, and the message of salvation as seeds. He spoke about four different soils in which seeds are sown.

The wayside soil: These are the people who listen to the good news of salvation and ignore it.

The rocky soil: These are the people who get momentarily excited about the good news of salvation, but do

Travelling Through Rough Waters

not count the cause, and when fiery trials of life come because their spiritual root was not deep down into the spiritual earth, they lose their faith.

The thorny soil: These people represent a special group of people in the church. They come to church, hear about the good news of the kingdom, get excited about it, and joyfully accept Christ as their personal savior. But as the days and weeks and months and years pass by, they get very busy with making a living and getting ahead, and their priorities get turned around. Their experience with the Lord gets choked with the cares of this world.

The good soil: These people listen to the good news of salvation and fully commit themselves to it. They live their lives in such a way that the good news has top priority in their lives, and they encourage others to become members of the commonwealth of heaven.

From the four groups Jesus mentioned, some of these people did not make it. These people came to the church with a sincere heart, but unfortunately, they got turned around by the deceitfulness of this world. Then Jesus went on to describe another group of people in the church who came, not to be saved, but to disrupt the church. These people were cognizant of what they were doing. They came as part of a destructive plan designed by the Devil. The Devil sends his own people to dwell among the people of the kingdom. These people know that they are been sent; they are not converted, but they enjoy the position that was given to them by the Devil.

Jesus started out by saying, "The kingdom of heaven is like a good man or an employer who left the city and

The People of the Kingdom

went out to the farm to sow seed. (When the world was young, there was much danger and instability in the communities. Most communities were fenced around with great walls and the husband would wake early in the morning and go outside the city to cultivate the field, and in the evening he would come home.) So Jesus said the man sowed seeds in the field and went back home for the night, but when it got dark, his enemy decided to destroy his field, so the enemy went and took some weed and sowed them all over the field among the good seed and then left. After a few weeks the seeds sprouted and the weed came up too. The workers saw it and told their employer. "We know that you gave us good seed to sow, but now the field is full of weeds. Where did they come from?"

The employer said, "My enemy did this to me." The employees said to the good man, "Let us go and pull up the weeds before they get too big." But he said to them, no, if I let you pull up the weed now, no matter how small they may be, you will pull up some of the good seed with them. So just let them all grow together and during the harvest time we will harvest both and then separate them, and when we have the wheat safely in the barn we will burn the weeds. For us to understand the story Jesus told, there are a few things I should explain. The goodly man or the employer in the story is God. The field or the vineyard in the story is the church. The good seed are the children of the kingdom. The enemy in the story is Satan and the weeds are tares or Satan's appointed agent in the church.

It is the Devil who sowed the tares in the church.

Travelling Through Rough Waters

Neither God nor His angels ever sowed a seed that would produce tares. Every tare, or weed, in the church was sent there by the Devil. The tares were sown after the good seed were sown and they were sown at night, meaning that after the gospel seeds were sown in the hearts of the believers, the Devil also came and introduced error and false principles. It was done at night, meaning that the person did not recognize what the Devil was doing to him or her. While both seeds are growing, they look alike. It is not easy to recognize them apart, even though so many think that they can easily tell the unconverted people in the church.

The Tares Have a Twofold Purpose in the Church

1. To endanger the wheat or church
2. To bring dishonor and ruining to the field or church

By bringing into the church those who bear the name of Christ while at the same time they deny His character, the Devil's aim is to dishonor the work of salvation and misrepresent God's name. The Lord must not be blamed for the fact that there are tares in the church. The world should not turn away from the church because there are tares in the church. The world will never be excused because there are weeds in the field. However, each member of the church is under a strong obligation to hold up the reputation of the church. The members of the church should not give the church a bad name. If you've got a problem that you are working with, please do it in secret—just between you and God. God would be more

The People of the Kingdom

pleased with you if you keep your problem just between you and Him while you are working on the problem.

It is the Devil's plan to let the members of the church take their problems to the world so that the world may speak evil of the church and find reasons not to accept the good news of salvation. The members of the church must be patient with the weak believers and be patient with those whom they branded as tares.

It should be noted that there is no record anywhere that because tares were in the field or the church, any wheat ever turned into tares. Members in the church who are not spiritual or fully converted cannot change the converted members to become unconverted. So be patient, they are not bothering you, they are bothering the cause of God, and if God can be patient, so can we.

The Wisdom of Letting Both Grow Together Until Harvest Time.

After a few weeks the seeds sprouted and the weeds or the tares came up too. The workers saw it and told their employer or the good man. "We know that you gave us good seed to sow, but now the field is full with weeds. Where did they come from?" "Let us go and pull up the weeds before they get too big." As the members of the church see true and false believers mingling in the church, they long to do something about it and, like the servants of the good man's household, they want to go and root up the tares. But the goodly man is wise; he tells his servant, now, leave them alone until the day of harvest, and today He also tells us, now, leave them alone until the day of harvest.

Travelling Through Rough Waters

Let us look at the reason why the Lord said to leave them alone: While the wheat and the tares are growing, the tares intertwined their roots around the good seed, and most of the time, if you pull out the tares you will also pull out the wheat as well. So the Lord said, "Let them stay together until harvest time, and I will send my angels to pull both and separate them." As the tares have their roots intertwined with the good seed, so false brethren in the church may closely link with true believers. The real characters of these pretenders are not fully manifested. Were they to be separated from the church, others might be caused to stumble, who but for this would have remained steadfast.

Many of the unconverted members in the church have a close relationship with converted members. They wrap their affections around them and they are closely knit together. Most people come to the Lord through others. Some people can only see God through others. So the Lord said, Don't interfere with the delicate balance. Let them grow together; I will do the separating. I see many people today trying to clean up the church by exposing evildoers in the church. That is destroying the cause of God. Now this does not mean that there is not a biblical procedure in dealing with open sin in the church.

But anybody who walks around and looks for sin in the church so that they may publish it is doing the work of the Devil. No one in the church should spread out the church's dirty linen. I take side with no one who seeks to expose the church's problems to the world. I believe that the Devil has sent men and women in this church to dishonor God's cause, but the Lord told me, "You

The People of the Kingdom

leave it alone, I will take care of it." And if you are truly converted, you need not worry about anything, because there is no place in history where it is recorded that a unconverted person ever changed a converted person to become unconverted.

People who leave the church because of this or that were not fully converted in the beginning. Nobody who is truly converted ever turns around and goes back in darkness. God has set the same principle in the church, which He Himself employed during the incident with Satan in heaven. He did not destroy Satan when he sinned. He was patient to let thing work itself out. There were angels and many other subjects at stake. They must see for themselves the true nature of the arch-deceiver and withdraw their affection from him. Through long ages God has borne the anguish of beholding the work of evil. He has given His infinite gift on Calvary, rather than leave any to be deceived by the misrepresentation of the wicked one; for the tares could not be plucked up without danger of uprooting the good seeds. If our God is able to endure such pain, shall we not be as forbearing toward the tares in the church? Shall we expose the church because of the tares as a way of revenge?

How Long Shall the Tares, or the Weed, Stay with the Wheat?

Until the end of the age. Until the end of probation. Embrace yourself because you will see them and they are going to vex your soul. You cannot walk around with a stick because you have no right to put them out. No one has a right to doubt the truth we preach because of

Travelling Through Rough Waters

the tares in the church. No one has a right to doubt the truth we preach because of the unworthy members in the church. No Christian needs to be disheartened because there are false brethren in the church. The church has always experienced tares among its members. This is nothing new for the church.

The church had to deal with liars and thieves like Ananias and Sapphira who came and joined themselves to the church. The church had to deal with witches like Simon Magus who was baptized and was functioning as a member in good and regular standing in the church. The church had to deal with members who had no interest in God's work such as Demas who considered himself as a member of God's church but forsook Paul when the going got rough. The church had to deal with men who wanted to use the church as a means to further their desire for prestige and fame such as Judas Iscariot who was numbered with the apostles. The church today has to deal with those who differ from the established doctrine of our church.

Tares in the church have always been a problem for the church, but the job of getting rid of the tares has never been given to the members of the church because the tares and the wheat closely resemble each other. I know that sometimes we think we can see clearly the wheat and the tares, but such a job is Divine and we must let it stay just where it is. This goes for the local members in the church; it goes for the pastor, elder, and deacon. It goes for the Conference, Union, Division, and General Conference. It goes for our publishing house and the E. G. White Estate. Let the wheat and the tares

The People of the Kingdom

grow together until the day of harvest. If somebody in the church behaves inappropriately, the Bible has given us a guideline of how to deal with that brother or sister.

The people of the kingdom are a unique set of people. In the heart of these people, spiritual nature and carnal nature are intermingled. The battle between God and Lucifer that started in heaven a very long time ago is still raging in the hearts of some of these people; nevertheless, if one wants to experience translation from this world to a world filled with beauty, peace, and joy, he is compelled to be a part of the people of the kingdom. This narrative reminds me that there is no safe place on the earth today; even the church of God is not safe. May God help us.

Chapter 9

Ye That Dwelleth in God shall Find Hope

The realities of life today have many people giving up, feeling confused, and sometimes wanting to curse God and die. The hills are hard to climb and the valleys are too wide. As we climb up the rough side of one mountain, it seems as if there are ten more mountains to climb. So, we find ourselves having premature gray hair, and the doctors are prescribing heart medication because of hypertension. The fun in life is so quickly gone

Ye That Dwelleth in God shall Find Hope

and we spend our days thinking about how to survive. Some people feel like staying home and resting for the day, but they can't because they also worry about missing a day's payout of the budget; thus, we sink deeper and deeper into our problem.

You and I must confess that sometimes we feel like giving up, forgetting everything, and if it were not for the grace of God many of us would do it. On March 25, 2008, the San Francisco Bridge in California was closed down for two hours. A man stopped his car in the middle of the bridge. He had a little child and a baseball bat in his hand. He threatened to bash the little child's head and jump off the bridge. For two hours the police tried to tell him that it wasn't worth it. If you and I don't have God, we, too, will jump. One pastor was awakened at 12:30 a.m. early one Monday morning by the insistent ringing of the telephone. "Pastor, this is Sarah, I've got a rope in my bedroom and I am going to kill myself tonight." "Okay, so why did you call me to tell me that?" replied the pastor. You and I both know that you can kill yourself anytime you choose, and neither God nor I can stop you if you desire to die.

Then the pastor recognized the cry for help and said to her, "Sarah, you do not have the talent to kill yourself. The last time you tried it you fell and broke your ribs. Can you wait until Friday to die?" "What are you trying to do? Stop me?" replied Sarah. "I am trying to find out if you can wait until Friday to die. We could have one last meal together, give each other a big good-bye hug, then you can go and kill yourself. What kind of fish would you like—tuna, snapper, or steak? Then she said, I will take

Travelling Through Rough Waters

the tuna fish. Sarah is not the only one who feels this way sometimes. Listen to David, the prophet of the Lord, in Psalm 22:14-25: "My strength and courage are gone, they have drained from my body like water from a broken jar. My arms feel as if they are out of their sockets and my heart feels as if it is made out of wax. My throat is as dry as the desert sands and my tongue sticks to the roof of my mouth. I feel as if you have left me lying in the dust to die." Even Jesus had his moment. In Matthew 26:38, he says, "Everything in my body is in turmoil. I am so weak I feel like I am dying, please stay with me." Life gets mean sometimes; however, beyond the dark clouds the sun is still shining. Remember that the darkest part of the day comes before morning. The songwriter said, "Never give up, Jesus is coming."

Someone said, "I have dreamed many dreams that never come true, but I have realized enough of my dreams to give thanks to God. I have prayed many prayers when no answers came, but answers have come often enough to my prayers to make me keep on praying. I have trusted many a friend who let me down, but I have found enough friends who are true. I have sown many seeds that fell by the wayside, but I have held enough golden shears in my hand to let me keep on sowing. I have drained the cup of disappointments and pain, but I have sipped enough nectar from the roses of life to make me want to live on." There is much hope for the child of God. Psalm 91 is a comforting psalm. He that dwelleth in the secret place of the Most High shall abide under the shadow of the Almighty.

Ye That Dwelleth in God shall Find Hope

The Protection of the Righteous

David said, "He that dwelleth in the secret place of the Most High shall abide under His shadow." In other words, anyone who has an intimate relationship with God can be at rest. It does not matter how intense our fear of the coming danger may be; we can be at rest. This is true, but we must believe it for it to work. Oftentimes for us to have this kind of faith in God, we must ignore some of what we see with our eyes and some of what we understand with our minds, because oftentimes faith and reality do not run parallel. It is paradoxical to tell me that the light and power man is coming to turn my light off, and he finally comes and turns the light off, and then you tell me not to worry about it, I've got light because the Almighty God is my protector. Some people have a problem with this kind of reasoning, but according to the expectation of the text, Christians are not some people. They are God's children and they have transcended the boundaries of the human domain into a realm that only the eyes of faith can dwell.

"Thou shall not be afraid of the terror by night nor for the arrow that flies by day nor for the pestilence that walketh in darkness" (Ps. 91:5). There is trouble everywhere; everything you attempt to do, there is trouble. Looking to find a Christian spouse? There is trouble. Trying to do a business? There is trouble.

Trying to do the right thing? There is trouble. Trying to find work? There is trouble. Even in the church, there is trouble. but the Bible tells us not to be afraid of trouble when we are trying to do the right thing. Press forward because you are dwelling in the secret place of the Most

Travelling Through Rough Waters

High. Someone said God is asking him to do something that he cannot do. I told the person, if God tells you to do anything it can be done.

Destruction at Noonday
The bombing of the World Trade Center. The constant war in every corner of the world. The HIV virus that is killing millions of people. TB and the list goes on. These are destructions at noonday. God said He will keep us because we are dwelling in the secret place of the Most High. Now, this special blessing only comes to those who make their dwelling place in God. The child who claims by words that he dwells in God will likely find himself or herself among the rest. These promises are for the faithful followers of God. In other words, you've got to mean business to get all of these blessings. This does not mean that Christians do not experience hardship and setbacks in this world, but God's special protection for His children should not be overlooked.

Why are the Righteous Protected?
Psalm 91:9 tells us, "Because you have made the lord your refuge and even the Most High God thy habitation." The righteous person is protected because he has made the Lord his dwelling place. Literally, where is the dwelling place of God that David is talking about in this passage of scripture? What is a dwelling place? Your dwelling place is where you live. Your dwelling place is where you sleep. Your dwelling place is where you eat. Your dwelling place is where you socialize. Your dwelling place is where you study. Your dwelling place is where

Ye That Dwelleth in God shall Find Hope

the family counsel together.

Your dwelling place is where you pray. So we conclude what David is saying here: If you live with God. If you eat with God. If you sleep with God. If you socialize with God. If you study with God. If you counsel with God. And if you pray to God, there is no need to worry when trouble comes because God cohabitated with you. Jesus was sleeping in the boat while the storm was raging; He was not worrying about anything because he was dwelling in the secret place of the Most High.

When the men who were possessed of demons and living in the graveyard charged down the mountainside after Jesus and the disciples, the disciples ran, but Jesus stood His ground because he was dwelling in the secret place of the Most High. When the waves are reaching higher and the water seems as if it is overflowing—the bills, the job, the business, schooling, and much, much, more—you still don't have a problem because you have made God your dwelling place.

I Will Send My Angels to Protect You

The Lion, that's the king of all beasts. The Adder, that's the poisonous snake. The Dragon, that's a sea monster. In other words, your problem could be as powerful and strong as a Lion, but don't worry, I can take care of it. Your problem may seem devastating and hopeless as a man bitten by a poisonous snake, but don't worry, I can take care of it. You may seem to be overwhelmed with your problems as a man who is overwhelmed by a sea monster, but don't worry, I can take care of it. I will send my angels to bear you up lest thou dash thy foot against

Travelling Through Rough Waters

the stones. I have sent my angels to bear thee up lest you crumple under the heavy load of life. God decided to do things for us, because we have set our love upon Him, therefore He will deliver us. "You can call upon me and I will answer you and I will deliver you. I will give you long life, and it is all because you know me" (Ps. 91:9, 14).

God Himself has made this promise to the church. God has never lied; therefore, this promise is still valid. Let us start living with God, sleeping with God, talking with God, praying to God, spending time with God, and allow Him to counsel us, then claim the promises of God. God seems to be a God that loves to have fellowship with His people. Not only does God want to have fellowship with people on earth, He plans to take us where He is living someday. Psalm 24:7-10 picks up the story. After Jesus's resurrection He took with Him representatives of the multitude who will walk on the sea of glass someday. Now, these are people who were raised from the dead at Jesus's resurrection (Matt. 27:52-53). When Christ died on the cross there was a mighty earthquake. We do not know how much it measured on the Richter Magnitude Scale, but it was a big one. The Bible says it was a violent earthquake, the ground shook and the top of the surrounding mountains broke off. This said the earthquake opened up the graves of the saints and when Jesus rose from the grave the following Sunday, these dead people rose from their graves too and went into the city to visit their loved ones. Paul tells us in Ephesians that these same people who rose from the grave with Christ went to heaven with Him (Matt. 27:50-53, Eph. 4:8).

Ye That Dwelleth in God shall Find Hope

Jesus Took to Heaven the Saints Who Rose from the Grave with Him

David gives us some insight as to what took place when Jesus the Good Shepherd got to the gates of heaven with the trophies of His victory on earth. The angels that were with Him said to the angels at the gates of heaven, "Lift up your head, O you gates! Be lifted up, you everlasting doors, the King of glory is coming in!" In other words, open up your everlasting gates of heaven, and let the King of heaven come in. The angels in heaven said, "Who is the King of glory?" And the angels with Jesus replied, "The Lord, strong and mighty, and He is mighty in battle. Open up, you gates, lift up, you everlasting doors, the King of glory is coming in!" The angels in heaven asked the angels on the outside again, "Who is the King of glory" The angels on the outside responded again, "The Lord of Host, He is the King of glory!"

The spirit of prophecy picks up the story. She said the angels were just having a good time, because they were so happy to see their commander and King. The angels asked the question a second time, "Who is the King of Glory?" And the angels on the outside responded, "The Lord strong and mighty, the Lord mighty in battle." Now, the original says it better, the original says, El-Shaddai, the Almighty God is standing on the outside with his children and He needs to come in. They asked the question again, and this time the angels with Jesus responded, "Jehovah El-Shaddai," the God who is, the God who was, and the God who will be. He is standing on the outside and He needs to come in (*The Desire of Ages*, 829-835; *Early Writings*, 187-191).

Travelling Through Rough Waters

The second response of Jehovah El-Shaddai functioned like a password that activated the computer which controlled inanimate objects, and the gates responded to the presence of their creator and flung themselves wide open. The gates could not wait any longer to obey the command of God. God's presence sent a signal to the gates and they opened themselves. Nothing can stop God and His children. After all our troubles and trials are over in this world, the Lord will take us home to live with Him.

When Jesus got to Heaven, there were cherubim (angels with four wings) and seraphim (angels with six wings); the representatives of the unfallen worlds were assembled. The heavenly council before which Lucifer had accused God and His Son were there, the representative of those sinless realms over which Satan had thought to establish his dominion—all were there to welcome the Redeemer. They were eager to celebrate His triumph and to glorify their King. But Jesus waved them back. Not yet; He could not receive the coronet of glory and the royal robe as yet. He entered into the presence of His Father. He pointed to His wounded hand, the pierced side, the marred feet, He lifted His hands bearing the print of nails. He pointed to the tokens of His triumph, He presented to God those raised with Him as representatives of that great multitude who shall come forth from the grave at His second coming. He approached the Father.

Before the foundations of the earth were laid, the Father and the Son had united in a covenant to redeem man if he should be overcome by Satan. They had clasped

Ye That Dwelleth in God shall Find Hope

Their hands in a solemn pledge that Christ should become the surety or guarantee for the human race. This pledge Christ has fulfilled. Upon the cross He cried out, "It is finished." The plan had been fully carried out. Now He declared, "Father, it is finished. I have done Thy will, O My God, I have completed the work of redemption. If Thy justice is satisfied, I will that they also, whom Thou hast given me, be with me where I am (John 19:30, 17:24; *The Desire of Ages*, 834). Those of us who suffer on the earth for Christ's sake will live with Him in paradise.

Chapter 10

The Mark of the Beast

Ever since I was a little boy, I was intrigued by the subject of the mark of the beast. There have been so many opinions on what is the beast, or who is the beast, and when will people receive this mark. I have decided to apply my reporting skills and look into this subject and inform my readers as to what I find. I thought that approaching the subject from a reporter's point a view would be a balanced approach, because a biblical reporter only tells what he finds and his readers make their own decisions based on the evidence. Please remember

The Mark of the Beast

that what I find could change your psychological equilibrium. I would like to start with the "beast." It only makes sense that if we are going to look at the mark of the beast, we should first identify the beast. Let us read the passages of scripture where this particular subject is taken from:

Then I was given another vision. I saw a huge beast which looked like nothing I had ever seen before come up out of the sea. In a way, it was similar to the dragon because it also had seven heads and ten horns, but this beast had ten crowns instead of seven, one on each horn. Blasphemous words against God were written on each head. This sea beast had the body of a leopard, the paws of a bear, and each head had the mouth of a lion. The dragon gave this beast its power, its earthly throne and great spiritual authority.

The dragon used this beast to deceive and kill God's people. "I saw one of the heads of this sea beast suddenly go limp as if it had been fatally wounded. This greatly affected the beast and it looked as if it would bleed to death. But suddenly the wound was healed and it was well again. Then I saw the beast begin to walk the earth. Everywhere it went, people were influenced by its charm. Soon they were worshiping this beast and said to each other, "Who is as powerful as this huge beast, and who would dare fight against it?" But they didn't realize that by worshiping the beast, they were worshiping the dragon that had given the beast its power and spirit. This sea beast made all sorts of religious claims for itself and even blasphemed God by claiming to speak for God. It exercised its power for forty-two prophetic months (or

Travelling Through Rough Waters

one thousand, two hundred and sixty years). It continued to blaspheme God and those who dwell in heaven by misusing His name and undermining the truth of His dwelling place in heaven. Then the dragon gave power to the beast to make war against God's people to overcome them. Soon it exercised its authority over every tribe, people, language and nation." Everyone on earth worshiped the sea beast, all those whose names had not been written in the Book of Life belonging to the Lamb of God who was willing to die for us even before this world was created.

Then I saw a large animal come out of the earth. It had two little horns like a harmless lamb, but it developed the power and spirit of the dragon and began to speak and act like one. This land animal began to listen to the sea beast. It decided to exercise its authority on behalf of the sea beast and to make everyone in the world worship the beast whose fatal wound had been healed. The dragon used this animal as a false prophet to perform incredible "miracles," such as bringing down fire from heaven for all to see. Then the land animal deceived people with false prophecies and with the miracles it could do with the dragon's help. It told the inhabitants of the earth to honor the beast that had been wounded by the sword but did not die. The animal threatened with death anyone who would not honor and worship the beast. It forced everyone, small and great, rich and poor, free and bond, to accept the mark of the sea beast on their right hand or on their forehead.

After this, no one could buy or sell unless he honored the sea beast by having its mark, which has its name and number. This calls for more than human wisdom, but with spiritual insight anyone can calculate its name and number, which is six hundred and sixty-six. It's a name and number made by man." (Rev. 13:1-18, *Clear Word Bible*)

As you can see, the chapter is loaded and mind-boggling. I will not look into every aspect of the chapter; however, I will look at the areas that help to clarify the subject under discussion. In prophecy a beast represents a kingdom (Dan. 7:23). Daniel 7:23 tells us, "The fourth beast shall be the fourth kingdom." Sometimes in prophecy, a beast represents a powerful leader. Revelation 5:6 describes Jesus (the spiritual leader of the Christian church) as a Lamb. Revelation 13:1 says that the beast came out of the water. Let me give a few prophetic definitions so that my readers may find it much easier to follow along with me. In biblical prophecy water represents people (Rev. 17:15). Earth in this context would represent a less populated area as compared to the sea, which would represent a more densely populated area. Wind represents war (Jer. 49:36-37). Horns represent kings (Dan. 7:24). So when John said the beast came out of the water he is referring to the fact that this beast, or power, was developed in the area of the world where it was densely populated with much people.

Let me go back into the passage and highlight a few things lest we forget what we have read. This sea beast would receive its power, and its seat, and its authority from the dragon (Rev. 13:2). Who is this dragon? The dragon is the Devil and Satan (Rev. 12:7-9). This sea beast would become a world power (Rev. 3:7). This sea beast is guilty of blasphemy (blasphemy means to claim power

Travelling Through Rough Waters

that belongs to God) (Rev. 13: 5,6). This sea beast has a mystical number, 666 (Rev. 13:18). This sea beast is a religious power (Rev. 13:5,8). This sea beast wars with and persecutes the saints (the ones who would not obey his command) (Rev. 13: 7). This sea beast is a religious system (Rev. 13:4). John said the people worship the beast. This sea beast makes war with God's people (Rev. 13:7). Daniel said this same sea beast changes God's law (Dan. 7:23-25). There is only one religious power on earth today that fits this biblical description and that is the papacy, or the papal system.

Prediction and Fulfillment

The Beast Received Its Power, Its Seat, and Its Authority from the Dragon

Let us look at a few highlights of this system. Revelation says the sea beast would receive its power, its seat, and its authority from the dragon (Rev. 13:2). By the way, why do we use the term sea beast? Well, if you notice in Revelation 13:1-10, John speaks about the beast he saw coming out of the water. Then in verse 11 he speaks about another beast that came up out of the earth. So there are two beasts and, to differentiate, we used the terms sea beast and land beast. Now, let us go back to the subject at hand. This sea beast would receive its power, its seat, and its authority from the dragon (Rev. 13:2).

Labanca, a professor of history at the University of Rome said, "To the succession of the Caesars came the succession of the pontiffs in Rome. When Constantine, a pagan emperor left Rome he gave his seat to the pontiffs."

The Mark of the Beast

Another statement taken from the Stanley's *History*, on page 40: "The pope filled the place of the vacant emperors of Rome, inheriting their power, prestige, and titles from paganism....Constantine left all to the Bishop of Rome....The papacy is but a ghost of the deceased Roman Empire, sitting crowned upon its grave."

When I tried to understand the statement John the prophet made in Revelation 13:2 with the historical data, I came up with the conclusion that when pagan Rome gave its power, prestige, title, and authority to the Church, it was Satan who was giving these features to the Church. Satan is the prince of this world, and he gives these to whomever he will, not to mention Satan cannot do business directly with people. He is not allowed to do that, so he used human beings who have committed themselves to him to do his work. Here is another statement:

The transfer of the emperor's residence to Constantinople was a sad blow to the presage of Rome; at the time one might have predicted her speedily decline, but the development of the Church and the growing authority of the Bishop of Rome, or the Pope gave her a new lease on life, and made her again the capital—this time the religious capital of the civilized world. (Abbot, *Roman History*, 236)

The Sea Beast Makes War with the Saints for Forty-Two Months

Revelation 13: 7 tells us that the sea beast makes war with the saints for forty-two months. In prophetic language, this time period works out to 1260 years, because

Travelling Through Rough Waters

a day in prophecy represents a year (Ezek. 4:6). The papacy persecuted the saints from 538 AD to 1798 AD. Nero, the fifth emperor of Rome, was the first to persecute the Church. Christians were falsely accused of the most dreadful crimes and declared to be the cause of great calamities, famines, pestilences, and earthquakes, but the blood of the saints watered the gospel. After Satan realized that his plan to persecute the saints was not accomplishing what he had wanted, he decided to trick them. Persecution ceased and instead there was temporal prosperity and worldly honor. The state became a friend of Christianity.

There was a compromise with the pure doctrine of Christianity. Idolatry were led to receive as part of the Christian faith, while they rejected other essential truths. They professed to accept Jesus as the Son of God and to believe in His death and resurrection, but they had no conviction of sin and felt no need of repentance or a change of heart. The church was in fearful peril. Prison, torture, fire, and the sword were a blessing in comparison to this. Some of the Christians stood firm, declaring that they would not compromise, but others were in favor of yielding or modifying some features of their faith and uniting with those who had accepted a part of Christianity, urging that this might be the means of the heathens' full conversion. Under the cloak of pretended Christianity, Satan was subtly manipulating and maneuvering himself into the church to corrupt their faith and turn the minds of the people from the Word of God.

Most of the Christians at last consented to lower their standard and a union was formed between Christianity

The Mark of the Beast

and paganism. Paganism, however, still clung to their idolatry, only changing the object of their worship to the image of Jesus, Mary, and the saints. Unsound doctrine, superstitious rites, and idolatrous ceremonies were incorporated into the faith and worship. The papacy today is the result of this union of paganism and Christianity. The 1260 years of persecution by the papacy came about because of this compromise. Those who would not surrender to this new compromise of mixed religion with paganism were severely persecuted from 538 AD to 1798 AD (The Great Controversy, p. 42-43).

The Beast Was Wounded
Revelation 13:3 tells us that one of the beast's heads was wounded. This happened in 1798 when General Berthier made his entrance into Rome, abolished the Papal Government, and established a secular one (*The Encyclopedia Americana*, 1941 ed.). This action of the French general slowed down the power and activity of the papacy. The beast's brutal force upon the people was broken for a while. The Bible says the beast was wounded, and this wound was inflicted by General Berthier.

The World Wonders after the Beast
Revelation 13:3 tells us that the world wonders after the beast. This is something that you and I see with our own eyes. Every place on the earth where the head of the papacy goes, the world wonders after him. Kings and priests, the wealthy as well as the poor, wonder after the beast.

Travelling Through Rough Waters

The Beast Blasphemies the Name of God

Revelation 13:5 tells us that the sea beast blasphemes the name of God. We stated previously that blasphemy means to claim power that belongs to God. Here are a few quotations that you could consider blasphemy from the beast or the papal system. "The Pope is of so great dignity and so exalted that he is not a mere man, but as it were God and the Vicar of God" (Ferraris, *Ecclesiastical Dictionary*).

Here is another quotation, "Seek where you will, through Heaven and the earth, and you will find, but one created being who can forgive the sinner...that extraordinary being is the priest, the Catholic Priest" (*The Catholic Priest*, 78-79).

I Timothy 2:5 tells us, "For there is one God and one mediator between God and man, the Man Christ Jesus." And in Luke 5:21: "Who can forgive sin but God alone. Another quotation, "We hold upon this earth the place of God almighty" (Pope Leo XIII).

We know that when any human being calls himself God, he blasphemes against God. Let me tell you a story to prove this. When Christ was on earth some of the Jews did not believe in Him. They did not believe that He was the Son of God, so one day Christ said it publicly that He was God. The Jews picked up rocks to hit Him. This is what they said: "For a good work we stone thee not, but for blasphemy, because you, being a man, make yourself God" (John 10:33). If Jesus had not been God, it would have been blasphemy to make such a claim. Here we see that any claim on the part of mere man to call himself God is blasphemy.

The Mark of the Beast

The Beast Tried to Change God's Law

Daniel was prophesying about this same beast in Daniel 7:25. Daniel said this beast would also think to change times and law (Dan. 7:23-25). Let us try to investigate and see if this is true. In Exodus 20:8-11 the fourth commandment reads, "Remember the Sabbath day to keep it holy. Six days shalt thou labor, and do all thy work, but the seventh day is the Sabbath of the Lord thy God. In it thou shalt not do any work, thou, nor thy son, nor thy daughter, thy manservant, nor thy maidservant, nor thy cattle, nor thy stranger that is within thy gates, for in six days the Lord made heaven and earth, the sea, and all that in them is, and rested on the seventh day, wherefore, the Lord blessed the Sabbath day, and hollowed it" (Exod. 20:8-11).

Let Us See What the Beast Did with This Law of God, Which Is Located in the Center of the Decalogue

"**Question,** Have you any other way of proving that the Church has power to institute festivals of precept?
Answer, Had she not such power she could not have done that in which all modern religionists agree with her, she could not have substituted the observance of Sunday the first day of the week, for the observance of Saturday the Seventh day, a change for which there is no Scriptural authority." (Rev. Stephen Keenan, *A Doctrinal Catechism*, 174)
"**Question**: What day was the Sabbath?
Answer: Saturday.

Travelling Through Rough Waters

Question: Who changed it?
Answer: The Catholic Church." (Rev. Dr. Butler, *Catechism*, Rev., 57)
"Question: Why do we observe Sunday instead of Saturday?
Answer: We observe Sunday instead of Saturday because the Catholic Church transferred solemnity from Saturday to Sunday." (Peter Giereman, *1948*, 50)

"Sunday is found not on scripture, but on tradition and is distinctly a Catholic institution." (*Catholic Record*, Sept. 17, 1893)

"The Pope has the power to change times and to abrogate laws and to dispense with all things, even the precepts of Christ." (Decretal De. Translat, Espiscap. Cap.)

"In A.D 364 many Christians were still observing the true Seventh-day Sabbath, The Lord's day which Christ made at creation. This is provided by the fact that the Church Council of Laodicea in the year A.D 364 forbade the observance of the Bible Sabbath, 'Christians shall not Judaize and be idle on Saturday, but shall work on that day, but the Lord's day they shall especially honor, and as being Christians, shall do no work on that day.'" (*History of the Councils of the Church*: from the original documents, Rev. Charles Joseph Hefele, D.D., Bishop of Rotenberg, book 6, section 93, canon 29, Vol. II, 316)

"The authority of the Church could therefore, not be bound by the authority of the scripture, because the Church had changed the...Sabbath into Sunday, not by the command of Christ, but by its own authority." (*Canon and Tradition*, 263)

The Mark of the Beast

Base on the above evidences, the papal system has changed the day of worship from the day God stated in Exodus 20:8-11 to Sunday the first day of the week.

The Beast Has a Number and It Is the Number of a Man

Revelation 13:18 said, the sea beast has a number and his number is 666. The official name or the Latin name for the head of the papacy, or the president of the papal system, is Vicarious Filii Dei, which has the numerical value of 666.

V — 5	F — 0	D — 500
I — 1	I — 1	E — 0
C — 100	L — 50	I — 1
A — 0	I — 1	
R — 0	I — 1	
I — 1		
U — 5		
S — 0		
TOTAL 666		

What Specifically Is the Mark of the Beast?

Let us go straight to the Catholic Church and ask this question and let them give us the answer. So we ask, "What is the Mark of the Beast?" And the Church said, "Sunday is our Mark of authority....the church is above the Bible and this transference of Sabbath observance is proof of that fact" (*Catholic Record*, Sept. 1923). "Of course, the Catholic Church claims that the change was her act....and the act is a mark of her ecclesiastical power and authority

Travelling Through Rough Waters

in religious matters" (Letter, dated Oct. 28, 1893, from C.F. Thomas Chancellor of Cardinal Gibbons).

So based on the above quotations, the mark of the beast is accepting Sunday observance or worship over the observance of God's Holy Sabbath day (Saturday), the day God commanded us to worship Him. This is powerful and scary. When one reads Revelation 13 without a deeper study, he or she will never understand what is going on. The prophet exposed the secret of the papacy and Satan. One may say, Don't you demonize the papacy, they are good people. This is not to demonize anyone. Some of the most beautiful people you can find today are in the Catholic Church; nevertheless, the prophecy of Revelation must be taken seriously. Most of the local people have no knowledge of what is going on in this system.

When Will People Receive the Mark of the Beast?

No one has the mark of the beast at this time. The mark of the beast will not be pronounced upon anyone until he or she has the opportunity to know about God's command then choose a man-made command over God's word. This matter is very serious. The land beast of Revelation 13 planned to kill anyone who refused to obey the command of the sea beast. Listen to this. This is the second beast of Revelation 13 speaking:

"The animal had power to breathe life into this image of the beast, and the nations of the world threatened with death anyone who would not acknowledge and worship the image of the beast. Everyone from the least

The Mark of the Beast

to the greatest, whether they were rich or poor, free or bond, were forced to accept the mark of the huge beast, either in their right hands by doing what it told them to do, or in their foreheads by acknowledging its authority. After this, no one could buy or sell unless he could prove his loyalty to the huge beast by having either the beast's mark or its name, which is its number." (Rev. 13:15-17, *Clear Word Bible*)

So, based on what I gather from Revelation 13, a person will receive the mark of the beast when he or she understands God's command; nevertheless, he chooses to accept the command of the papacy over the command of God. For example, in Exodus 20:8-11 God commanded worship on the seventh day, but the papacy changed God's command and instead commanded people to worship on the first day of the week (Sunday). When a person understands God's Command and willingly disobey, that person is in danger of receiving the Mark of the Beast.

Before I close I want my readers to take a second look at the following questions and answers:

Question, Have you any other way of proving that the Church has power to institute festivals of precept?
Answer, Had she not such power she could not have done that in which all modern religionists agree with her, she could not have substituted the observance of Sunday the first day of the week, for the observance of Saturday the Seventh day, a change for which there is no Scriptural authority." (Rev. Stephen Keenan, *A Doctrinal Catechism*, 174)

Travelling Through Rough Waters

Question, what day was the Sabbath day?
Answer, Saturday
Question, who change it?
Answer, The Catholic Church. (Rev. Dr. Butler, Catechism, Rev. 57

What I noticed, Satan and God have been into an age-old battle over worship. Satan wanted worship and God said worship belongs to God and God alone. Ezekiel 28:14-17 tells us about Satan when he was in heaven. This is what it said:

"You were the anointed angel, the one who stood at my right hand. You lived with me on my holy mountain and walked in the fire of God's presence. You were flawless and blameless from the day I created you until sin sprang up in you, and you became evil. Your nature change, and you were filled with jealousy and violence. You spread evil to all who would listen. So I expelled you from heaven, and you fell from the holy mountain of God. I had to force you to leave my presence even though you had stood next to me. You had become proud of your wisdom and beauty. Your high opinion of yourself led you into sin, and you rebelled against me. You let the beauty and wisdom I gave you corrupt you, so I cast you out of heaven and you walked the earth in shame."

Revelation 13:4 tells us that the people were worshiping this beast and said to each other, "Who is as powerful as this huge beast, and who would dare fight against it?" But they didn't realize that by worshiping the beast, they were worshiping the dragon that had given the beast its power and spirit. So Satan is deceiving the people; they

The Mark of the Beast

think that they are worshiping the beast, but it is Satan who wants worship. That is why he gave his power, seat, and great authority to the beast (Rev. 13:2).

Everything that has to do with the mark of the beast has to do with worship. Now, if we could take a quick glimpse into heaven with the eyes of the mind, we would notice that a battle between Christ and Satan started in Heaven (Rev. 12:7). Satan was able to get the angels involved in this power struggle between him and God. Satan lost the battle. Ezekiel said he was cast out of heaven, and both he and the angels who joined him were thrown out of heaven. We do not know how many angels there are in heaven, but the Bible says that one-third were thrown out with him (Rev. 12:4). Now, Satan comes to earth and continues with this same battle, and now he his dragging the human family into it. The angels who were thrown out with Satan lost their position in heaven. The mark of the beast is similar to the act of throwing the angels out of heaven. The mark of the beast will be placed upon people who take sides with Satan or obey his command instead of God's command. The battle started with worship and it will end with worship. The battle started in heaven, and the final round will be fought out on planet earth.

Where Will the Beast's Mark Be Placed on People?

Revelation 13:16 tells us that the mark is placed in the right hand or on their forehead. The right hand refers to the ability to work. Anyone who refuses to obey the command of the beast will not be able to buy or sell,

Travelling Through Rough Waters

they will not be able to work and make money to support themselves or their family. The forehead refers to the will or the mind. Everyone will decide for or against God. The mark of the beast is a serious matter. Before the mark of the beast is placed upon anyone, he or she will have already made the decision whether to obey God or the Devil. The mark of the beast will be received based on our observance of Sunday over the observance Sabbath (Saturday), the day God commanded us to worship Him. When every man makes his decision, then the mark will be placed upon mankind. Please be advised that people who receive the mark of the beast will not be saved, because they have already decided against God. Just like the angels who decided against God were thrown out of heaven.

The mark was placed in the forehead, which refers to the seat of the will. The people who receive the mark of the beast are given the chance to think about what he or she is doing. Mankind understands that all worship belongs to God. It really doesn't make any difference whether it is the beast or the Devil, mankind should not be worshiping either of them, because all worship belongs to God. The papacy changed God's day of worship, because Satan wanted God to understand that when the people worship on Sunday, they are not worshiping Him; instead he (Satan) gets the worship because he (Satan) has commanded them to worship on Sunday, and this type of reasoning makes sense.

God told the people to worship Him on Saturday (Sabbath) (Exod. 20:8-11). Satan came along through the papacy and changed God's command and the people went

The Mark of the Beast

right ahead and followed through on Satan's command to worship on Sunday instead of Saturday. Revelation 13:14 says, when the people did this, they were worshiping the dragon or Satan. They went to church on Sunday, and they were sincere, but Revelation said they were worshiping the Devil, because it was the Devil who gave them the command to worship on Sunday. Some people say it really does not matter what day you worship God, but in this case it matters, because you have God, and another creature wants your worship, and whomever's command we follow shows our allegiance.

Who Will Receive the Wrath of God?
Revelation 14:9-10 tells us that the wrath of God will fall upon the people who decided against God and received the mark of the beast. Those who will receive God's wrath in the last days are those who receive the mark of the beast. God decides who is to be saved based on whose servant we are (Rom. 6:16). Jesus said if you are not with me you are against me (Rom. 6:22). To be certain that no one receives the mark of the beast, God said we should keep His commandment and the faith of Jesus (Rev. 14:12).

I believe the mark of the beast is a very serious matter. I notice that God has taken time out of His busy schedule in running the universe, and has sent a message to planet earth in regard to the subject of the mark of the beast. This is what He said:

[A]nd I saw an angel flying high in the air, proclaiming one last time the eternal gospel to every nation, tribe, language and people. He called out in a loud voice for

Travelling Through Rough Waters

all to hear, saying, "Honor God and glorify His name, for the time has come for His judgment to begin. Worship Him who created the heavens, the earth, the sea and the springs of water."

I saw another angel flying behind the first one, and he, too, gave his message in a loud voice for all to hear, saying, "Babylon! Confusion! There is a falling away from truth because the sea beast is working to make every nation drink the intoxicating wine of its spiritual adulteries." I noticed a third angel flying behind the first and second ones, and he also gave his message in a loud voice for all to hear, saying, "Those who worship the sea beast and its image and agree to receive the mark of its name on his forehead or on his hand will have to drink the wine of God's judgment, which will be poured out unmixed with mercy from the cup of His indignation. This will take place in the presence of the holy angels and of the Lamb. The fire of God's judgment will not rest until those who worship the sea beast and the animal and have the mark of its name are totally destroyed." (Rev. 14:6-11, *Clear Word Bible*)

John stresses the point that the angels delivered the message in a loud voice, which indicates that the message is important and everyone on the earth needs to hear this message because the subject of the mark of the beast will affect everyone who is living on the earth. Those who receive the mark of the beast will die in the lake of fire. Revelation 14:11 tells us, "The fire of God's judgment will not rest until those who worship the sea beast and the animal and have the mark of its name are totally destroyed." Satan will also die in the

The Mark of the Beast

lake of fire. Ezekiel 28:18 tells us that God will bring fire down on Satan and reduce him to ashes in the sight of all those watching. The sea beast will die in the lake of fire. Revelation 20:9 tells us, "And the Devil who had deceived them was thrown into the lake of fire and consumed together with the sea beast, the land animal, and all the wicked." I hope that I have helped to stimulate your spiritual appetite to study more on this vital subject, and not only to study, but that you will make sure that you do not receive the mark of the beast.

Chapter 11

The Armor of God

There are a lot of people today who have strange ideas about going to heaven. I heard a story about a professor who died and when to heaven. When he got to the gates of heaven Peter stopped him and said, "Well, I know that you have done a very good work on earth, establishing schools and helping others to get an education, changing their lives for the better, but I just cannot let you go into heaven like that, that is not enough. Okay, I am going to give you a break, but you've got to do three things for me.

The Armor of God

a. Tell me how many seconds in a year.
b. Tell me how many T's in a week.
c. Tell me what is God's name.

The professor scratched his head and said, You pick the hardest ones for me, old Peter. He went away for a while and came back to Peter and said, I got the answers. Peter said, All right, tell me how many seconds in a year? The professor said, Twelve. January 2nd, February 2nd, March 2nd, April 2nd and so on. Peter said, you are pretty smart. All right, tell me how many T's in a week? The professor said, "Two. Today and tomorrow." Okay. Tell me what is God's name? The professor said, "Haword." Peter said, how did you come up with that? The professor said, It is right there in Matthew: "Haword Father which art in heaven Howard be they name." Peter opened up the gates and he went in, but I declare to you today it is not that easy to go to heaven.

In Romans 7:24, Paul called sin, "the body of death." In Bible days, when a person commits a serious crime against the State or the country, such as treason or tries to overthrow the government. The authorities would give that person the worse punishment. The authorities would go to the morgue and get a dead body and strapped the dead body to the person, and body would stay strapped to the living person until it rots and the worms from the dead body feed on the living person's body until he dies. According to Paul, sin is like a dead body that is strapped on to a living person and the person cannot get rid of it. Therefore, Paul tells us to fight against sin and do not allow sin to take control of us, but

Travelling Through Rough Waters

before you fight you should take unto you the whole armor of God.

Going to Heaven Is Not about Being Smart, It Is about Fighting

When we fight we prepare to fight. A good example in the preparation for a battle is the United States in the Gulf War. I took a glimpse on the Internet to see the kind of military hardware the United States was using in the Gulf War ten years ago, and this is what I came up with:

The AGM-88 Harm—this is a high-speed anti-radiation missile aircraft carrier. It carries a warhead of 150 pounds and travels over 760 miles per hour. I saw the S-3B Viking. This is a fighter jet that searches for and destroys submarines. It flies 500 mph with a radar that covers a 2600-mile range. Then I saw the 6B Prowler. This piece of equipment is used to jam and disrupt an enemy's radar and communication system so that US Aircraft can hit their target without been detected. I saw the U-2 high-altitude day-and-night surveillance spy plane. She flies about 70,000 feet above sea level with an average speed of 472 mph. Then I saw the E-3 Sentry all-weather surveillance command control and communication center flying at a speed of 360 mph. This aircraft is a mobile communication system. She flies around while monitoring the communicating between Washington, the Gulf, and anyplace in the world at the same time.

I thought that I was finished, but then I looked and saw the C-130 Workhorse, which provides vital logistical support. She takes off and flies at 33,000 feet above

The Armor of God

sea level with a payload of 100,000 pounds. There were still more. The KC-10 Extender carries over 356,000 pounds of jet fuel. She can deliver 470 gallons of fuel per minute while flying at a speed of 619 mph. And the F-117A Night Hawk Tactical Fighter Jet—this is the only plane in the world of its type. She flies at a high subsonic speed faster than sound. I could not help but notice the A-10 Thunderbolt flying at a speed of 420 mph. She flies close to the ground with a 30mm 6g gelatin gun and a laser-guided missile bomb weighing up to 16,000 pounds.

By this, you would think that it should be enough, but I saw the F16 CJ Fighter Falcon. She flies at 1500 mph with an M61 20mm multi-barrel cannon. Air-to-air missiles. She performs with crisp dexterity and maneuverability. I also noted the F15 Eagle—the world-leading, superior, all-weather tactical fighter jet traveling at a speed of 1875 mph, with a radar covering over a 3450-mile radius. Not to mention the Support Ship. The Navy's largest combat logistics ship. It has the speed and maneuverability to keep up with the Carrier Battleship. She carries over 177,000 barrels of oil, 2,150 tons of ammunition, 500 tons of dry stones, and she has the ability to redistributes these items simultaneously to the Carrier Battleship.

I scrolled down the screen and looked at the vastness of their ammunition. The troops are numberless. The United States is ready for battle, and it makes no difference what anyone may say, we are ready for battle.

Paul was in prison in Rome when he wrote Ephesians chapter 6. He looked around him at the soldiers who were guarding him, and I believe the Holy Spirit directed

Travelling Through Rough Waters

him to write this portion of the book using the soldiers' dress code and even his own spiritual battleground experiences. He recognized that, like the soldiers, Christians are fighting a battle and they should take the fight seriously and dress themselves and prepare for the occasion. If we are going to win this battle with the Devil, we need to dress up in our spiritual armor, because Satan is not about to lose this battle; like the USA, he comes to kill and he comes to win. The first thing Satan does to assure his victory, he uses the soldiers of the army he is fighting against to fight their own people. This may sound ridiculous, but look at most of the battles in the church, it is not the people of the world who come and fight against the church, it is the people in the church fight among themselves.

We saw Nero, who was the fifth emperor of Rome, persecuting the church, but his persecution was not even a drop in the bucket compared to the church persecution of their own people for 1,260 years (538 AD to 1798 AD). We saw the Philistines going up against the church, but most of the time the church defeated them, except for when the church went against God's command and He punished them by allowing their enemies to defeat them. Satan found out that it is better when the church fights each other. When Satan cannot get enough people in the church to do his dirty work, he sends his own people in the church, so they come and get baptized and take their permanent place in the church, then start to do their father's work. So you will notice that the church does more harm to the church than the world does harm to the church.

The Armor of God

The battle is secure, but for us individually, we must fight to win. We will lose if we do not put on the spiritual armor and fight to win. Through the agency of the Holy Spirit, Paul instructed the Christians how to fight and he provided us with the dress code.

The Belt of Truth (Ephesians 6:14)

The first piece of equipment in the spiritual armor is the Belt of Truth. If you go on the battlefield without your proper attire, your movements will be hampered, so you need your belt to be tightly fitted around your waist. The Belt of Truth is nothing more than the Word of God firmly fitted in your mind so that you may not vacillate about what you believe. Before you tell the good news, you should at least believe it yourself. You should know what you believe and then believe it. Don't let anybody turn you around, stay focused. The first thing a Christian should do as he or she enters the service of God is to study and know God's word.

New believers, you will not last in this church if you do not study your Bible. The Word of God will give you strength to continue your Christian walk with God. As the physical belt keeps your pants around your waist so that it does not fall off (today almost everyone's pants are falling off, but normally, the pants are supposed to be at the waist), so the Word of God, like a belt firmly fitted in your mind, will keep you from falling. Some of us do not wear the belt anymore and we have fallen by the wayside. Put on your belt, go to Bible study, and find out what God wants you to know. If you do not know God's word you will not last in the church.

Travelling Through Rough Waters

The Breastplate of Righteousness (Ephesians 6:14)

In Greek it's called, "The Heart Protector." When you are in battle you want to make sure that the vital organs are protected; a sword could easily pierce your heart and the fight would be over, so you've got to cover your heart with a breastplate. The Christian Breastplate is the Righteousness of Christ. Christians have got to cover up with the righteousness of Christ when they fight. If they are not covered up, they will get hit from every side. Sister Brown is going to hit from the back and you are going to tell her a piece of your mind and leave the church. At the job you will get hit from the side, and you are going to sacrifice principles to keep your job. The wife or husband will hit you from the front, and you are going to get mad and stop supporting the family and going to church. But if you are covered up with the righteousness of Christ you will say, Lord, I want to tell Sister Brown a piece of my mind, but I am supposed to be covered up with the blood of Christ, so I've got to just pinch myself and smile as if everything is all right.

The Spiritual Shoes (Ephesians 6:15)

You need good shoes, so you may be able to stand firm when you fight. Soldiers wear the best and strongest shoes. The Spiritual Shoe is our strong determination to stand firm on the Word of God. As physical shoes give soldiers a firm grip as they travel over rough ground, the spiritual shoe, likewise, gives Christians a firm grip on the truth, so they may stand firm on the Word of God. Yes, you may tell me many things, but I have read

The Armor of God

for myself the scripture and I know what God wants me to do. Have you ever seen some folks who are tossed about by every wind of doctrine that comes their way, and somebody comes and tell them one thing and they listen. Another person comes and tells them something else and they listen, and by the time they are finished they have lost their mind trying to listen to everything people tell them.

The older Jamaican people used to say they are just "wishee washee", which means they cannot stand on what they believe. The reason why they are tossed about is because they are not wearing their spiritual shoes. The spiritual shoes will give us a firm grip on the Word of God. Put on your shoe and wear it every day, study God's word every day. Time is winding up and you got to keep your eyes on the Lord; some of the preachers you cannot even trust anymore, so you must learn to know God for yourself.

The Shield (Ephesians 6:16)
The shield was used in battle to catch the fiery darts of the enemy. Fiery darts were made of combustible materials that were ignited on the head of the arrow, so it would set on fire whatsoever it came in contact with. Some people are like combustible materials. They will ignite and set the church on fire, not the Holy Ghost fire, but the fire of destruction. Paul said, Faith is the Christian's Shield to catch the fiery darts that the Devil sends our way to set us on fire. The Christian shield is like the US 6B Prowler, which jams and disrupts the enemy's radar and communication system, so that the

Travelling Through Rough Waters

Christian can get on with the business of Christ without interruption. The Devil sends fiery darts at Christians by way of Discouragement, Disappointment, Impatience, Ungodly brotherly behavior Slander, lying, malicious behavior, Envy and anger, Lying, gossiping, and false finding, and if we do not have our shield, these fiery darts will set the church ablaze and burn like wildfire, but with our shields outstretched we will say to the disappointments, "Though He slay me, yet will I trust Him." We will say to discouragement, "Weeping only lasts for a while, but joy comes in the morning." We will say to the lying lips, "Father alone will know all about it, Father alone will understand why, cheer up, my brother, live in the sunshine, He will deliver us in the sweet by and by."

The Helmet of Salvation (Ephesians 6:17)

The helmet is to cover the head. Soldiers ought not to go on the battlefield without their helmet because it protects the most vital part of their body. You do not want to loose your head in the heat of the battle. You must be sharp, keen, alert, and ready for action. Do not let the enemies confuse you. Stick together and plan wisely. The Helmet of Salvation refers to the "Seat of the will." One's salvation depends on the right action of the will. Our will protects and guarantees our salvation. The Christian must be sharp, keen, and alert. He cannot be vacillating as to what he is going to do in regards to his salvation. He must say like David, "O God, my heart is fixed and I am ready to go where you want me to go and I am ready to say what you want me to say."

We ought to fix our minds on Jesus no matter what

The Armor of God

others may say. My mind is made up and you cannot turn me around. There is a story about a mother and her son. The son said to his mother: "I am tired of hearing you talking about this God. Who is He? What has He done for you? Can you see Him? Can you touch Him?" The mother said, "No, my son." Then he said, "How then do you know that He exists? Do not tell me anything more about this God business." And he went off to bed; but later on that night the Holy Spirit helped out that poor old mother.

In the middle of the night the boy cried out, "Mother, come quickly, I am feeling much pain. I've got a toothache and it is hurting me so bad, I don't think I will live to see daybreak." The mother paused for a moment, then she said, "Son, can you see the pain? "No, Mother, but I know it is there." "Can you touch the pain?" the mother said to her son. "No, Mother, but it is there, get me something quick." The mother said, "Earlier on this evening you asked me, how do I know that God exists? You asked me, could I see Him? Could I touch Him? And I told you no. But, you see, it is just like the toothache; you cannot see the pain, you cannot touch the pain, but you know that it is there, because you feel it. So it is with my God. I cannot see Him, I cannot touch Him, but I know that He is there, because every now and then I can feel Him moving in my soul." You and I know that God exists, because every now and then we can feel God's Spirit moving in our soul. Somebody said, He woke me up this morning and I just talked to Him today.

Travelling Through Rough Waters

The Sword (Ephesians 6:17)
Finally, Paul said you need a sword. Even though the United States has all that state-of-the-art equipment, they need men on the ground for hand-to-hand combat missions. So Paul said you need a sword. The soldiers always keep their swords with them, just in case they find themselves into a close corner and need to cut their way out. Today you will say "shoot" your way out. If you notice, the sword is the only part of the armor that is both defensive and offensive. The sword is the Word of God. Rightly using the Word of God, you will be able to stand face-to-face with your enemy and fight (and that's defensive) and with the word you will be able to drive back your enemy (and that's offensive).

Let Me Tell You a Story about the Word
Some years ago I was teaching a Bible class at a certain prison. That particular night the subject was on the state of the dead. I told the prisoners, when a person dies he does not go to heaven or hell, he goes into the ground and that's it until Christ comes. One of the prisoners got up and said to me, "Mr. Teacher, that is not true because the Bible supports the idea that when a righteous person dies he goes to heaven." And he pulls out Revelation 6:9-10: "And He opened up the 5th seal and I saw souls under the altar who were beheaded for the name of Christ, and cried with a loud voice, saying how long, Lord, are you going to take to avenge our blood of them that dwell on the earth" (Rev. 6:9-10).

    He had me backed into a corner so I grabbed my sword and came out swinging. I went all the way back

The Armor of God

to Genesis 4:10 and I said, Look, brother, if you can tell me what is going on in Genesis 4:10, I will tell you what is going on in Revelation 6:9-10. God asked Cain, Where is your brother? Cain said to God, Do I look like my brother's keeper? God said, You are lying, your brother's blood cries out to me from the ground. Now, does Abel's blood have a mouth? God said, His blood cries out to me.

I said to the brother the essence of what is going on here in this passage of scripture in Revelation 6:9-10 and Genesis 4:10 is nothing more than reality crying out to God. It is justice demanding that something be done for the crime that has been committed against these people. Cain cannot get away with what he has done to his brother. In Revelation 6:9-10 the papacy and all its confederates cannot get away with what they have done to the children of God during the 1,260 years of persecution (538 AD to 1798 AD). The Sword will help you cut your way out of every circumstance.

Then Paul said, after you have finished dressing up in the armor of God, you ought to stand your ground. You ought to plant your feet firmly down and stand for Jesus. You ought to stand when life seems not worth living. You ought to stand when it seems as if God refused to answer your prayer. You ought to stand when friends and loved ones turn their backs on you. You ought to stand when life does not seem to make sense anymore. You ought to stand when it seems as if there is no need to keep on living. You ought to stand like Jesus stood in Gethsemane when the human destiny trembles in His Hands. You ought to stand when you do not feel like

Travelling Through Rough Waters

standing anymore. You ought to stand and fight because your salvation depends on you fighting the battle of Life. And when all is said and done, stand for Jesus. May God give us grace to keep on fighting, and when our days on earth are ended He will say to us, well done, my good and faithful servant. You have fought a good fight. You have kept the faith. Come and enter into my joy.

Chapter 12

Dead Man Walking

What happens to the dead? We go to church and pay our last respects to the dead and then we go home, but what really happens to them? We watch the funeral home lay our loved ones to rest, but what happens to them? Where are they? Are they in heaven? Are they in hell? Does the righteous man go up to heaven when he dies? And the wicked man goes to hell? Is it good-bye for all eternity? Or do they come back to see us every now and then? The Bible asks the question, "If a man dies shall he live again?" Broken in spirit, sad and

Travelling Through Rough Waters

lonely, we often wonder why it should be thus all day long. Why should we be deprived of our loved ones?

Let us see if the Bible has anything to say about the state of the dead. Genesis 2:7 tells us, "And the Lord God formed man out of the dust of the ground and breathed into his nostrils the breath of life, and man became a living soul." Mankind came from the dust (we are nothing but dirt). Some of us act so high and mighty, but we are nothing but dirt, and everything about us is dirty. In Job 16:22, the prophet made it very clear that when he dies, he is not coming back. "When a few years are come, then I shall go the way whence I shall not return."

"A man is appointed once to die, but after this the judgment" (Heb. 9:27). "My breath is in me, and the spirit of God is in my nostrils" (Job 27:3). The spirit of God in Job's nostrils is referring to his breath in his nostrils. The word Spirit is translated from the Hebrew word "Ruah," which means breath. Ezekiel 18:4 tells us, "The soul that sinned, it shall die." Please note that the soul can die. A soul does not live forever. Some religious leaders tell their congregation that the soul lives on after the person dies, especially if the person was a godly person, but Ezekiel said, "The soul that sinned shall die." Human beings are mortal and mortals die. The King James Version uses the word soul 1,600 times, but never once uses the term immortal soul, which indicates that a soul does not live forever.

Dead Man Walking

What Happens When a Person Dies?
   a. The body returns to dust (Gen. 3:19).
   b. The spirit (breath) returns to God who gave it (Eccles. 12:7).

Oftentimes the word spirit is used synonymously with breath in the Bible. So in this case, the breath returns to God who gave it. Note that the text did not say the soul returns to God. It states very clearly that the spirit or breath returns to God. The breath is the air we breathe and when we die the air we breathe returns to the One who gave it.

   c. The person's thoughts perish (Psalm 146:4).

When a person's thoughts perish, this person does not know anything. He or she cannot speak because the mind is not working. He or she cannot see because the mind is not working. He or she cannot go anywhere because the mind is not working. "Their love, hatred, and jealousy are all gone because the mind is not working, never again do they have a part in anything that's going on in this world" (Eccles. 9:6). So their feelings perish, their love perishes, and their hate and envy perish. If a man hates you and he dies, your trouble with him is over. There is nothing he can do to you again. "His son (children) comes to see him and he does not know" (Job 14:21).

Can the Spirits of the Dead Speak?
The dead cannot praise God (Psalm 115:17). So the dead are not in church nor are they in heaven, because they

Travelling Through Rough Waters

cannot praise God. The dead cannot speak because their thoughts have perished. If a man cannot think, he will not be able to speak. A man's tongue manufactures what the thoughts tell it to manufacture, so if the thoughts perish the person will not be able to speak. So when I hear my departed loved ones speaking, who is it that is speaking? We will get back to this later.

Can the Dead Communicate with the Living?

We go to the burial ground to see the graves of our loved ones, but can they see us, can we really talk to them? The dead cannot communicate. Those persons who family members and friends claim they saw—who are they? They may look like our departed loved ones. They may sound like our departed friends. Their perfume may even smell like our departed loved one's perfume, but they are not our loved ones, they are the spirits of devils (Rev. 16:14). Psalm 146:4 tells us that when a person dies his thoughts perish; therefore, the dead person knows nothing. Based on the Word of God, the dead person does not know where he used to live. He does not have a mind to think. He does not know that he or she is dead. He or she does not know his children. He does not know his former friends. He does not know where he is buried. He cannot bring his family a message from the dead because he cannot speak. He cannot give dreams to his loved ones about the lottery, so if a person said he or she saw a departed loved one, that person would not be speaking to or seeing his or her departed loved one, he is speaking to the spirit of devils.

Dead Man Walking

Demons are the best impersonators in the world, not to mention demons know everything about us. Demons are not omnipresent, but they communicate among each other. When Satan was thrown out of heaven, he took one-third of all the angels with him to planet earth (Rev. 12:4-9). These are the same angels we call demons today. No one knows how many demons are in this world, but we know that they are many. When Christ was on earth He healed a demon-possessed man. Christ asked the demon who was controlling the man for his name. The spokesman for the demons spoke up and told Christ that his name was Legion for they were many (Mark 5:1-9).

A legion in the Roman Army was one thousand; as we noted before, no one knows how many demons came from heaven with Lucifer, but Satan has enough demons here on earth that he can afford to send as many as one thousand demons to one person.

Modern Spiritualism

Modern spiritualism started in the United States in 1848 with the Fox Sisters, who stated that there was no death. This statement is a direct defiance to God's word in Genesis 2:17: "Ye shall surly die." God told our first parents that if they eat from the forbidden tree they would die; however, the Fox sisters said that there is no death. The Fox sisters were three sisters from New York who played an important role in the creation of Spiritualism here in the United States. Margaret, Kate, and Leah Fox, from 1814 to 1892, played an important role in the development of spiritualism in the US. The

Travelling Through Rough Waters

two younger sisters used "rapping" to convince their much older sister and others that they were communicating with spirits. Their older sister then took charge of them and managed their careers for some time. They all enjoyed success as mediums for many years. In 1888 Margaret confessed that their rapping had been a hoax, but spiritualism continued as if the confession of the Fox sisters had never happened (Wikipedia, Fox sisters).

"And when they shall say unto you, seek unto them that have familiar spirit [meaning, if somebody tells you to go to the psychic, the palm readers, or witches] you should say, should not a people seek unto their God?" The living going to the dead? (Isa. 8:19). God's people should have nothing to do with those who communicate with the spirits of darkness. "To the law and to the testimony, if they speak not according to this word it is because they have no light in them (Isa. 8:20).

When a Person Dies He Goes Back to the Dust Where He Came From

Dust + Spirit = Living Soul, or the Elements of Earth + Breath = A Living Being.
Dust - Spirit = A Corpse, or the Elements - Breath = A Corpse. "As the cloud vanishes and is gone, so he who goes down to the grave does not return" (Job 7:9,10).

I will try to use a light bulb to demonstrate to you the state of the dead. If you have a light bulb in your house you may try this demonstration yourself. Please go to the light switch on the wall and turn on the light. Then turn off the switch and you will notice that the light is gone. Then ask yourself, where is the light? What happened to the light? Someone may tell you that you are losing your mind, because you turned off the power then are asking for the light. Well, you are not losing your mind. It is true that you turned off the power, but the power is not the light. Where is the light? Well, you do not know what happened to the light, so I shall tell you. The light ceases to exist.

You had light because when you switched the power on and the light bulb made a connection and the result was light. When you turned off the power, you broke the connection and the light ceased to exist. The same thing happens when a person dies. A living soul is a combination of the elements of earth plus the breath of God. When the dust and the breath of God made a connection, man became a living soul. When the breath of God and the dust or the elements of the earth separates, man ceases to exist. Nothing has gone anywhere. Just like the light, nothing goes anywhere; it just ceases to exist.

A person stops living because the breath is gone from his body. There is no special entity of human being that can live when the breath is taken away from him. Psalm 146:3-4 says, "Put not your trust in princes, nor in the son of man, in whom there is no help. His breath goes forth, he returns to his earth; in that very day his thoughts perish. No one leaves the grave and goes anywhere; all of us will remain in the grave until Christ comes."

I empathize with those who have lost their loved ones. I know what it felt like to lose your loved ones. I have lost my mother, I have lost my father, I have lost my sister, I have lost my brother, I have lost my niece,

Travelling Through Rough Waters

and I have lost my nephew. I have felt the pain death has dealt to the human family, but I have not given up hope in God's word, because I Thessalonians 4:13 tells me, "But I would not have you to be ignorant, brethren, concerning them which are asleep, that ye sorrow not, even as others which have no hope." Don't behave as if you have no hope. For those who trust in God, and accept Christ as their personal Savior from sin, death is a temporary separation. I Corinthians 15:51-52 tells us, "Behold I show you a mystery, we shall not all sleep, but we shall be changed. In a moment, in the twinkling of an eye, at the last trumpet: for the trumpet of the Lord shall sound, and the dead in Christ shall rise incorruptible and we shall be changed.

Jesus will burst through the clouds of heaven with all the holy angels with Him. He will come back to earth to gather all the sleeping saints and take them home with Him. He will come and the angels will gather the saints together. I Corinthians 15:53 tells us, "For this corruptible shall put on incorruptible, and this mortal must put on immortality." If you are in your office working, you will see Him coming. If you are sick in the hospital, you will see Him. If you are taking a vacation on the 747, you will see Him coming. If you are flying in the Concorde, you will see Him coming. If you are riding on the monorail, you will see Him coming. If you are the president of the United States, you shall see Him coming. Nothing will stop the great God of the universe to come and get the sleeping saints.

Your father who died in the Lord will get up out of his dusty bed. Your mother who died in the Lord will get

Dead Man Walking

up out of her dusty bed. Your child who died in the Lord will come forth. Your husband who died in the Lord will get up out of his

dusty bed. Your sister who sleeps in peace today will come forth. They will be carted up to meet Him in the air. It won't be long before we see Him in the air.

My daughter loves this part of the story. When I am making a presentation on the second coming of Christ, she always tells me, "Daddy, say it like the way you told us before." Then I would say, according to *Early Writings*,

It was at midnight that God chose to deliver His people. As the wicked were mocking them, suddenly the sun appeared, shining in his strength, and the moon stood still. The wicked looked upon the scene with amazement, while the saints beheld with solemn joy the tokens of their deliverance. Signs and wonders followed in quick succession. Everything seemed to turn out of its natural course.

The streams ceased to flow. Dark, heavy clouds came up and clashed against each other. But there was one clear place of settled glory, whence came the voice of God like many waters, shaking the heavens and the earth. There was a mighty earthquake. The graves were opened, and those who had died in faith under the third angel's message, keeping the Sabbath, came forth from their dusty beds, glorified....The sky opened and shut and was in commotion. The mountains shook like a reed in the wind and cast out ragged rocks all around. The sea boiled like a pot and cast out stones upon the land. And as God spoke the day and the hour of Jesus's coming and delivered the everlasting covenant to His

Travelling Through Rough Waters

people, He spoke one sentence, and then paused, while the words were rolling through the earth. The people of God stood with their eyes fixed upward, listening to the words as they came from the mouth of Jehovah and rolled through the earth like peals of loudest thunder. It was awfully solemn. At the end of every sentence the saints shouted, "Glory! Hallelujah!"

Their countenances were lighted up with the glory of God, and they shone with glory as did the face of Moses when he came down from Sinai. The wicked could not look upon them for the glory. And when the never-ending blessing was pronounced on those who had honored God in keeping His Sabbath holy, there was a mighty shout of victory over the beast and over his image. I saw the pious slave rise in victory and triumph, and shake off the chains that bound him, while his wicked master was in confusion and knew not what to do; for the wicked could not understand the words of the voice of God. Soon appeared the great white cloud, upon which sat the Son of man. When it first appeared in the distance, this cloud looked very small. The angel said that it was the sign of the Son of man. As it drew nearer the earth, we could behold the excellent glory and majesty of Jesus as He rode forth to conquer. A retinue of holy angels, with bright, glittering crowns upon their heads, escorted Him on His way. No language can describe the glory of the scene.

The living cloud of majesty and unsurpassed glory came still nearer, and we could clearly behold the lovely person of Jesus. He did not wear a crown of thorns, but a crown of glory rested upon His holy brow. Upon

Dead Man Walking

His vesture and thigh was a name written, King of kings, and Lord of lords. His countenance was as bright as the noonday sun, His eyes were as a flame of fire, and His feet had the appearance of fine brass. His voice sounded like many musical instruments. The earth trembled before Him, the heavens departed as a scroll when it is rolled together, and every mountain and island were moved out of their places.

And the kings of the earth, and the great men, and the rich men, and the chief captains, and the mighty men, and every bondman, and every freeman, hid themselves in the dens and in the rocks of the mountains; and said to the mountains and rocks, fall on us, and hide us from the face of Him that sitteth on the throne, and from the wrath of the Lamb: for the great day of His wrath is come; and who shall be able to stand?" Those who a short time before would have destroyed God's faithful children from the earth, now witnessed the glory of God which rested upon them. And amid all their terror they heard the voices of the saints in joyful strains, saying, "Lo, this is our God; we have waited for Him, and He will save us."

The earth mightily shook as the voice of the Son of God called forth the sleeping saints. They responded to the call and came forth clothed with glorious immortality, crying, "Victory, victory, over death and the grave! O death, where is thy sting? O grave, where is thy victory?" Then the living saints and the risen ones raised their voices in a long, transporting shout of victory. Those bodies that had gone down into the grave bearing the marks of disease and death came up in immortal health

Travelling Through Rough Waters

and vigor. The living saints are changed in a moment, in the twinkling of an eye, and caught up with the risen ones, and together they meet their Lord in the air. Oh, what a glorious meeting! Friends whom death had separated were united, never more to part. On each side of the cloudy chariot were wings, and beneath it were living wheels; and as the chariot rolled upward, the wheels cried, "Holy," and the wings, as they moved, cried, "Holy," and the retinue of holy angels around the cloud cried, "Holy, holy, holy, Lord God Almighty!" And the saints in the cloud cried, "Glory! Alleluia!" And the chariot rolled upward to the Holy City…. (285-288)

What a day this will be. I look forward to this glorious time. It is my desire that everyone who reads this book will be in that number when Jesus comes to gather the saints.

Chapter 13

City in Space

About two hundred years before King Tut ruled Egypt, the Israelites were in bondage, pressed into servitude by a new line of pharaohs. In fact, it was probably Thutmose I, the same pharaoh who built the first hidden tomb in the valley of the kings. The king became alarmed by the strength of the Hebrew people and commanded that every male firstborn child should be thrown into the river Nile (Exodus 1:22). At the very time of this decree a son was born to a Hebrew family, Amram and Jochebed (Exod. 6:20). Determined that their little baby

Travelling Through Rough Waters

boy should not die, they hid the child for three months. Fearing that they would get caught with the child, they made a watertight basket and carefully placed it into the river. Miriam, the baby boy's sister, stayed close by to see what would happen to her brother. Soon a princess, with her servant girls, came to the river to bathe, and they saw the basket floating in the river among the bulrushes and she instructed her servant girls to fetch the basket and bring it to her. She quickly saved the infant's life and decided to adopt him. Since she had no male heirs to the future throne, this child would become the ruler after her father died. And so she named the baby boy Moses (which means "drawn out of the water") (Exod. 2:10).

When Miriam saw how tenderly the princess held the child, she ran and asked her if she needed a nurse for the child. The princess agreed and Miriam went and got the child's mother to care for him. During the early years of Moses's life, his mother recognized that she only have a short time to spend with her child, so she taught Moses to obey and trust the God of heaven. Then from their humble home Moses was taken back to the royal palace where he become the son of the princess.

I believe at the palace, Moses received the highest education, both civil and military training. Moses was in line for the future throne, and all the wealth, influence, and power of the civilized world lay at the feet. It was his for the taking, if he cast his lot with the Egyptians and forgot the God of heaven. The palace of Pharaoh would be his home. The valley of the kings would be his final resting place. His body would be wrapped in a hundred yards of fine linen when he died and placed in the valley of the

City in Space

kings (he might have been a mummy today).

But Moses chose something better than the valley of the kings for his final resting place. Hebrew 11:24 -26 tells us, "By faith Moses, when he became of age, refused to be called the son of Pharaoh's daughter, choosing rather to suffer affliction with the people of God than to enjoy the passing pleasures of sin, esteeming the reproach of Christ greater riches than the treasures in Egypt, for he looked to the reward." Moses looked for a city whose builder and maker is God.

Moses was looking beyond the gates of the palace, he was looking beyond the pleasures of this world to a land that is fairer than day, and by faith we all can see it afar, because our Father waits over the way to prepare us a dwelling place there. The songwriter says, "In the sweet by and by we shall meet on that beautiful shore." I myself look forward to a land that is fairer than day, a land where trouble will be no more, a land where sickness will be no more, a land that we call the sweet by and by. While the relics of Egypt were impressive, they could not compare with the future that Moses chose.

On Mount Sinai, God cried out to Moses, Moses take off thy shoes from off thy feet, because the place where you are standing is holy ground. Moses moved on to the top of Mount Nebo and there he died alone, without a royal funeral, without fame and wealth. This is an unfair exchange you may say, but not so, my friends. I Corinthians 2:9 tells us that Moses knew that our eyes have not seen, our ears have not heard, neither has it entered into the hearts of man the things which God has

Travelling Through Rough Waters

prepared for them who love Him. Moses was not buried by the dignitaries of Egypt. He did not receive a royal salute, but angels left their bright home in glory and came all the way to planet earth and buried the body of Moses when he died (Exod. 34:5-6). Jesus came all the way from glory to get the body of Moses. Jude 9 tells us that Satan and all the demons told Jesus that He could not get the body of Moses because he was a sinner. Jesus said to them, Get out of my way, Satan, I have plucked him from the miry clay and planted his feet on the rock to stand.

This reminds us of ourselves. Sometimes we are trying to be our best, and Satan comes and whispers in our ears words of discouragement, "You are not a child of God." But tell him to get thee behind you, tell him to get out of your way so that you can serve your God. You and I may have to go through our Red Sea, but just like the children of Israel, we will make it to the promised land. Matthew 25:34 tells us there is a city prepared for the children of God and we each have a mansion in that city. Abraham, Moses, Elijah, and many more had their eyes fixed on that city whose builder and maker is God. John said, He saw the city, He called it the new heaven and the new earth (Rev. 21:1). The first heaven and the first earth passed away, and there was no more sea. John said, "And I heard a loud voice in heaven saying, behold God came down to earth to live with man. And God and the people of earth shall be one. They shall see His face and His name and character shall be in their mind every day (Rev. 22:3).

The plan to bring heaven to planet earth started a long ago. The second person of the Godhead planned two

City in Space

personal and special trips to planet earth. After which He planned to bring heaven to planet earth. For the first trip He came alone to die, but on the second trip He will bring the entire family with Him, then after which the Godhead plans to relocate to planet earth and bring the city with Him. Let me give you a glimpse of how the first trip ended and how the second trip will begin:

I would like you to come with me on the wings of your imagination back to Abib (April) AD 30, about 3:00 p.m. in the afternoon. Jesus died on the cross. His death was the major focus on the evening news. He died at 3:00 pm and was buried that same evening. No autopsy was done, maybe the note they put into His file was "There was a battle and there was a casualty." Romans guards who feared no mortals kept watch around the graveside all through the night. Satan did not trust the mighty hands of humans, so he commanded thousands of evil spirits to keep guard around the graveside of the Savior. The prince of darkness was the commanding officer at the graveside. If it was possible, the prince of darkness and his apostate army would have kept forever sealed the grave where our savior was laid (*Desire of Ages*, 778-779); but while Satan dispatched his army of angels at the graveside, God also dispatched holy angels who excelled in strength to keep watch around the sepulcher, waiting to welcome the Prince of Life.

I can imagine that Satan wrote the name of our savior in the Book of Death at 4:00 p.m. Friday evening. Five o'clock, six o'clock, seven o'clock, eight o'clock, nine o'clock, ten o'clock, eleven o'clock, twelve o'clock, the Savior's name was still in the book. Saturday morning came and Satan

Travelling Through Rough Waters

did not go to church (I am assuming that Satan goes to church on Sabbath sometimes). The situation was too intense; it made no sense going to church, his mind would not be on church today. At sunset on Saturday, it seemed as if the time was going by so slowly. Satan had a fever, temperature about 200 degrees Fahrenheit, B/P 300/250 respiration 50. Sweat ran down his face like great drops of blood. It was now approaching midnight and maybe he called out to one of his attendant, "Can you tell me if His name is still in my book of death?" "Prince of darkness, Christ's name is still there," replied his attendant, "he is not going anywhere." About 1:30 a.m. the prince of darkness cried out, "Look again to see if His name is still there!" "Don't worry yourself, prince of darkness, we've got this man under control." About 3:00 a.m. the prince of darkness told his attendant to check again, and the attendant told the prince of darkness, "His name is still there, but it seems as if the letters are fading; but don't worry, maybe my eyes are fooling me or maybe the kind of paper we used to write His name was not the best brand." "Make sure you check up on all the other evil spirits to make sure all of them are okay," replied the prince of darkness. Early Sunday morning, Lucifer said, "Do you feel something? Check the book!" The attendant replied, "Prince of darkness, I saw the place where His name was, but His name is erased from the book of death."

 David said God laughed after Satan's plan to keep the Prince of Life in the grave (Psalm 2:1-4). Had it been possible, the Prince of Darkness with his apostate army would have forever sealed the tomb that held the Son of God, but a heavenly host surrounded the sepulcher. Angels that excelled in strength were guarding the tomb, and waiting to welcome the Prince of life (*Desire of Ages*, 779).

God the Father dispatched Gabriel from the throne, and a beam of God's glory went before him to illuminate the pathway. When Gabriel's feet touched down on planet earth, the earth could not handle such power, and it shook and tossed about like a drunken man. Gabriel rolled back the stone, stooped down on his knees, and said, "Jesus, come forth. Thy Father calls Thee" (*Desire of Ages*, 778).

Jesus got out of the tomb and stayed around for forty days. The dead bodies that came back to life and lived in their immortal bodies, went into the cities and told their living relatives what had happened (Matt. 27:52-53). They, too, stayed with their friends and loved ones for forty days; then Jesus called them all together and informed them of the time they will be taking off for heaven. Jesus, the living saints, and the angels were now ready to take off. They went to the Mount of Olives and there they transcended to heaven.

David tells us in Psalm 24 what happened when they got to heaven. They got to the gate of the city and the angels and the saints who were with Christ told the angels on the inside of the city to open the gate so the king of glory may come in. Who is the king of glory? asked the angels on the inside. He is the Lord! replied the angels and the saints. Open up ye gates, ye everlasting doors, both angels and saints shouted another time. Who is the king of glory? asked the angels on the inside

Travelling Through Rough Waters

another time. The original said that the saints and the angels responded the third time, "His name is Elohim" the Mighty God. He is a ruler and a mighty warrior and all things both in heaven and on earth respond to his command. At this time the gates, though an inanimate object, responded to the command of Elohim and, like a heavenly remote control system, they flung themselves wide open so that the Creator and Sustainer of all things may come in.

The inauguration service started in heaven. Jesus was anointed. There was also an anointing service taking place on earth at the same time; we call it Pentecost. The Pentecostal service is part of the inauguration service that was going on in heaven. As Jesus was being anointed by the Father and the Holy Spirit to take up His priestly duty in heaven, so His disciples on earth were also being anointed by the Holy Spirit to join with Him in completing the final phase of redemption.

Jesus said, "This gospel of the kingdom shall be Preached for a witness in all the world and then shall the end come." Daniel 7:9-11 tells us that, in 1844 Jesus moved into the Most Holy place of the heavenly sanctuary and the work of the investigative judgment began. Daniel states, "I saw ten thousand times ten thousands stood before Him, the books were opened and the judgment was set (Dan. 7:9-11). But it is not over; Jesus is coming back in power and glory. I Thessalonians 4:16 tells us that Christ will come back to earth very soon. He will descend from heaven with a shout. He will command the sleeping saints to get up out of their dusty beds. Then those of us who are alive and remain will be

City in Space

changed and together with the resurrected saints we will be caught up in the sky to meet our Loving Savior in the air. And from then on we shall all be with Him.

The Christians who serve God do not serve Him for nothing; there is a glorious day ahead of us. John said, I saw a new heaven and a new earth (meaning the old earth with all its polluted atmosphere was gone, and the oceans, which take up almost two-thirds of the earth's surface, were no more. The earth was now back to the way God made it in the beginning). John continued with the vision: I saw the Holy city, the New Jerusalem (beautifully dressed) coming down out of heaven from God. John also heard a loud voice coming from the throne saying God will personally live with His people and be with them. They will be a part of the royal family of heaven and God will truly be their God (Rev. 21:1-8). John was very careful in describing the city for his readers. He said, "The city has 12 foundations. The city is 1200 furlongs or 1500 miles [375 miles on every side]. The wall of the city is made of Jasper. The streets of the city are made of pure gold (Rev. 21:14,19). There is no need of any light and power companies, because the Glory of God shines in the city. I want to be in that city; don't you? Come and go with me to my Father's house.

> There will be no sickness in that city.
> There will be no blind people in that city.
> There will be no deaf people in that city.
> There will be no paralytics in that city.
> The dumb will speak in that city.
> There will be no darkness in that city.

Travelling Through Rough Waters

> There will be no bodies with HIV in that city.
> There will be no guns in heaven.
> Jesus will be the light of the city.

Lying days will be over, cheating days will be over, and killing days will be over in that city. We will walk in the light, the beautiful light in that city.

There is a river in that city, and they called it the river of life (Rev. 22:1). The river runs from the throne of God, and when we drink the water from the river we will be drinking life, because it is called the river of life.

John also said there is a tree by the side of the river and they call it the tree of life. The tree bears twelve different types of fruit for the year. Every month the tree bears another fruit (Rev. 22:2). That's for those people who get tired of eating the same fruit all the time. God is mindful of every little thing. Isaiah 11:6 and 9 tells us a few things about that city as well. He said, "The leopard shall lie down beside the little children in that city" (Isa. 11:6-8). There will be no more death in that city. There will be no more crying on Mount Zion because Jesus shall wipe away all tears from our eyes. There will be no need of light and power in that city because Jesus will be the light of the city. Jesus is thinking of you in that city. Jesus is waiting for you in that city. Jesus died for you, so that you could go to that city. Jesus is knocking at the door of your heart, so that you can go to that city. Beautiful flowers in that city. Beautiful landscaping in that city. You can take an evening walk with Jesus in that city. There will be no sunset in that city. The old order of things will pass away. Evil is gone. Sin is no more. The angel told John, "Write down everything you saw, because it is true" (Rev. 22:6).

Chapter 14

The Father – The Son – The Holy Spirit

The Government of God
The name God is not the name of a person; it is the name of the Divine Immaterial Substance. There is only one God (Deut. 6:4, Isa. 44:6). However, God exists in three persons, the Trinity. God the Father. God the Son. And God the Holy Spirit. The Father is a person. The Son is a person, and the Holy Spirit is a person (the Bible says when He the Holy Spirit is come)

The Father – The Son – The Holy Spirit

(John 14:26, 16:8-13). All three persons of the Godhead interacted at the baptism of Christ (Matt. 3:16-17). "As soon as Jesus was baptized, He came up out of the water and knelt on the riverbank to offer a prayer of thanksgiving. As He looked up, heaven itself seemed to open. Then the light of the Holy Spirit descended like a dove and hovered over His head. And a voice from heaven said, 'This is my Son whom I love. I am very pleased with Him'" (*Clear Word Bible*). So we see Jesus coming out of the water, the Holy Spirit descending like a dove over His head, and the voice of God the Father saying, "This is my beloved Son in whom I am well pleased."

All three persons of the Godhead are involved in a person's baptism (Matt. 28:19-20). "So go and tell people of all nations the good news and baptize them in the name of the Father, the name of the Son, and the name of the Holy Spirit. Teach them everything I've taught you. I'll always be with you, even until the end of the world." All three names of God are mentioned at a person's baptism. All three persons of the Godhead are involved in the process of sanctification (John 14:26). "The Holy Spirit whom the Father will send to represent me, will help you understand these things more fully after I'm gone and will help you remember what I've said." So the first person of the Godhead sends the third person of the Godhead to help people understand what the second person of the Godhead says. All three persons of the Godhead cooperate in saving man from sin.

Travelling Through Rough Waters

The Attributes of God
When we speak of the attributes of God, we are speaking of the essence of God's being. What God is. His traits and character. The attributes of God are divided into two sections:

a. The relative attributes refer to how God functions.
b. The absolute attributes refer to who God is.

The Relative Attributes of the Godhead
The Godhead Is Eternal (Exod. 3:14, Ps. 90:2, Rev. 1:8). The Godhead has no beginning and He has end.

The Godhead Is Omnipresent (Jer. 23:23-24, Rev. 1:8).
The Godhead is everywhere present. This is not pantheism, which claims that God is in everything and everything is God.

The Godhead Is Omniscient (Job 37:16, Ps. 139:2-4, 147:4-5, Isa. 40:28, Rom. 11:33).
   The Godhead knows Himself and everything else. He knows the past, present, and future perfectly. He can look at the past, present, and future at the same time, but when He deals with mankind He behaves within our level of understanding.

The Godhead Is Omnipotent (Rev. 19:6, Jer.32:17, Job 42;2, Psa. 107:25-29).
   The Godhead does what He will. Nothing is too hard for the Godhead to do (Jer. 32:17). The Godhead does

whatever He will to do in heaven and on earth. With the Godhead, all things are possible (Matt. 19:26, Dan. 4:25,35).

The Godhead Is Immutable (Mal. 3:6, Sam.15:29, Psa.33:11, Isa. 46:10-11,

James 1:17). The Godhead is unchangeable The Godhead is perfect; He cannot change for the better or for the worse.

The Absolute Attributes of the Godhead
Now let us look at the absolute attributes of the Godhead. The absolute attributes of God refer to who God is. It is what constitutes God's being.

The Godhead Is Holy (Ps. 99:9).
God's being is holy at all times and anything He touches becomes holy. Let me give you an example. Exodus 3:1-5 tells us a story about Moses's encounter with God: "One day Moses was taking care of the sheep and goats of his father-in-law Jethro, a priest of the Lord in Median, when he took them across a stretch of wilderness to graze near Mount Sinai. Here the Angel of the Lord spoke to him from the middle of a burning bush. When Moses first saw the bush on fire, he wondered why it didn't burn up. "That's strange," he thought. "I'm going up there to see what's going on." So Moses went up the slope, and as he approached, the Lord called out from the middle of the fire, "Moses! Moses!" He answered, "Yes, here I am." "Stop!" the Lord said. "Don't come any closer. Take off your sandals, because you're standing on holy

Travelling Through Rough Waters

ground." Now, this mountain had been there for a long time, sheep and goats with their caretakers for many years have been upon this mountain and there was no problem, but as soon as God showed up on the mountain it became holy and Moses could not approach it. We conclude that God is holy and anything He touches becomes holy or destroyed at once.

The Godhead Is Righteous (Ezra 9:15).
Everything that God does is righteous even when He kills His own creatures. God cannot be unrighteous. God's being is righteous. We understand righteousness to be a state of mind, but if a person should touch God, that person would just touch righteousness. When the second person of the Godhead took on human flash and lived on earth, He never allowed evil thoughts to enter His mind. I noticed that even on the cross when evil men did all manner of evil to Him, just before He died He prayed for them. He asked His Father to forgive the people who were putting Him to death. This is righteousness in action.

The Godhead Is Just (Rev. 15:3, 22:12).
God knows how to be just, because He is justice. He cannot be unjust because His nature is just. When mankind tries to be just, they are reflecting God's nature. Satan sinned while he was in heaven (Ezek. 28:12-17). God threw him out of Heaven and he could not go back to heaven. Mankind, on the other hand, sins and God forgives them and plans to take them to heaven to live with him. Only a just God could make such a

The Father – The Son – The Holy Spirit

decision. The unjust man who thinks that he is just would say God's decision is partial, but anything that has to do with sin cannot be found in God, because He is righteous and just. Isaiah 55.8-9 tells us, "My thoughts are not your thoughts, neither are my ways your ways. As the heavens are higher than the earth, so are my thoughts higher than your thoughts and my ways higher than your ways."

The Godhead Is Mercy (Isa. 55:7).
God is merciful even when He destroys the wicked. One of God's absolute attributes is "Mercy." God is merciful to all His creatures and shows mercy to His creatures. God shows mercy even to evil spirits. The Book of Mark 5:1-13 tells a story where Christ had mercy on one thousand demons. Jesus and His disciples went across the lake to the province of Decapolis, not far from the city of Gadara. As soon as Jesus and the disciples set foot on the beach, one of two madmen living in a graveyard charged down the hill, heading straight for Jesus and the disciples. It was clear to everyone that he was demon-possessed. They had been living among the empty tombs for sometime. When the authorities had arrested the most aggressive one, he broke his chains and escaped. Because this had happened so often, the authorities finally gave up and left him alone. Day and night he would terrorize people traveling that hillside road, screaming at them and cutting himself with sharp stones until his body was covered with blood.

Now he came charging down the hill directly at Christ, and the disciples turned and ran, but Jesus stood His

Travelling Through Rough Waters

ground. When the man came near Jesus, he suddenly fell on his knees as if to worship Him, then shouted, "What do you want with me? You are Jesus, Son of the Most High God! In the name of God I ask you not to torture me!" Before Jesus cast the demons out of the man, He said, "Tell me your name." One of the demons answered, "I don't have one name; I have many names because we are many." The KJV says, "My name is Legion for we are many" (a legion in the Roman army was one thousand). Then the spokesman for the demons pleaded with Jesus not to make them leave that part of the country. On a nearby hill was a large herd of swine. The demons begged Jesus, saying, "Please let us go into the pigs and possess them." Jesus gave them permission, and the demons came out of the men and went into the pigs and all the pigs jump into the sea and drown themselves. So even demons enjoy God's mercy (*Clear Word Bible*).

The Godhead Is Love (John 4:8, Jer. 32:3).
God loves those that He destroys (those whom God destroys He still loves them). God does not know how to love, He is love. The wicked who will be going to Hell, it is not that God does not love them, but they have chosen to turn away from their loving Savior. God does not hate sinners, He hates the sin. The person who will be going to hell is like a man who works very hard and saves up money to buy a house, but one day the house catches on fire, and someone comes along and says to the man, "The house is on fire. Get out." The man says, I am not getting out, I bought this house and I am not about to give it up, so the house finally burns up and the

The Father – The Son – The Holy Spirit

man gets burnt up in the house. Jesus is after sin, not people, but some people will not let sin go. They love sin dearly, so they get burned up with sin. Someone said, If you try to write the love of God on a parchment, it would stretch from sky to sky, and if the ocean was ink and it is used to write the love of God, it would drain the ocean dry.

The Godhead Is Gracious (Titus 2:11).
God does favors for us that we do not deserve. The wages of sin is death, but He pardons us and dies instead for us. Grace is a favor that we do not deserve; however, God gives us grace. God loves to do favors for people, because that is His nature. Even when people do terrible things, God extends His grace to them. Nebuchadnezzar was emperor of the first world power (Babylon), and he started bragging about his skills and ability to control the whole world. God sent a message to him and told him to stop bragging because God gives power to whomever He will, but Nebuchadnezzar ignored God and continued to brag about his power and ability. One day he was standing upstairs in his palace, and started to think about his power. He did not speak; only the thought was in his mind and he heard a voice that said to him, "King Nebuchadnezzar, your kingdom has been taken away from you. You will be driven from the society of man and you shall live with the animals and eat grass as the ox" (Dan. 4:29-33). Nebuchadnezzar was driven from his palace for seven years, but God was gracious to him and restored him back to his position as emperor.
The Godhead Is Truth (John 5:20).

Travelling Through Rough Waters

God does not lie, He cannot lie, He does not have anyone to lie to. (When you say God is truth, we are talking about Truth that can be touched.) God tells us not to lie to one to another, because He is trying to develop His character in us. He wants us to be like Him. No family likes to have a liar living with them, even if he is a family member. God plans to take us to His home to live with Him and He wants us to stop lying before He takes us home. This is not going to be easy for God, because some people believe their own lie. They have lied so many times, now they believe their own lie. But God will give us grace; and because nothing is too hard for God to do, He will continue to give us His grace until we see the need to tell the truth and nothing but the truth.

The Godhead Is Pure (Hab. 1:13).
Sin makes us impure, but God has no sin; therefore, He is pure. Anything that is not pure is consumed in His presence. 2 Thessalonians 2:8 tells us that when Christ comes, His presence or His brightness shall kill the wicked. People who are not pure cannot stand before a holy God. 2 Thessalonians 2:8: "The Lord will destroy him with the breath of His mouth and by the brightness of His coming."

There is a difference between the relative attributes and the absolute attributes. The relative attributes tell us how God functions, but these attributes have no control over Him; in other words, if God does not want to be omnipresent, these attributes have no control over Him. We saw Christ did this when He came to earth. Christ emptied Himself when He came to earth (Phil. 2:7). He

The Father – The Son – The Holy Spirit

emptied Himself of omnipresence, He emptied Himself of omniscience. He emptied Himself of omnipotence, just to mention a few. He emptied Himself of these attributes and depended upon the first person of the Godhead to supply Him with what he needed. The absolute attributes, on the other hand, are the essence of God. God cannot stop being love. He cannot stop being just. He cannot stop been merciful. If God should have a substance so to speak, it would be His absolute attributes.

Jesus Is God

Jesus was preexisting with God the Father before the world was (John 17:5). Jesus and God the Father share the same glory (John 1:10). Jesus made the universe, He made the angels including Lucifer, He made you and me (John 1:3.). "All things were made by Him, and nothing that was made was made without Him." So the same person we call Jesus was the same person God the Father was speaking to in Genesis 1:26 when He said, "Come let us make mankind in our own image."

Anyone who does not believe that Jesus is God does not understand the definition of the word "God." The name God refers to the Divine Immaterial Substance and Power that exists in three persons, the Trinity. God the Father. God the Son. God the Holy Spirit. The second person of the Godhead is unique; He is now different from God the Father and God the Holy Spirit. The second of the Godhead has two natures: the nature of God and the nature of man. He made this choice because of His love for us.

Please remember when we say God the Father tells

Travelling Through Rough Waters

Jesus to let them make man in their image, this idea does not necessary mean that we look like God physically. God is a spirit, and spirit has no flesh like human beings. Man was originally made like God with certain limitations. Man was made in the image of God in respect to his intelligence. God is the super mind; He is the infinitely intelligent One. As for God, nothing has to be for anything to be, for God said let there be and there was. Man is like God in that he is also gifted with intellectual powers by which knowledge is acquired. He is capable of creating thoughts, and recognizing thoughts that were suggested as well as imposed upon his mind.

Man was made in the image of God in respect to his moral nature. God's being is holy and righteous as far as God is concerned. If He wants, He could let us touch righteousness and holiness. Anything God touches becomes holy. God is infinitely pure and divinely happy in His life. Man was made in the image of God in righteousness and holiness. He was made with a disposition to be happy and to promote happiness on planet earth and the universe.

Man was made in the image of God in respect to his position. God is the Supreme Ruler of all things in heaven and the earth. Both angels and men are His subjects. Both animate and inanimate objects are under His authority. Man reflects the likeness of God in that he was made to be the ruler or the king of planet earth. He was made to have dominion and power over the earth. Man was made in the image of God in respect to the fact that he has the power to exercise love and affection. The Bible tells us that God is compassionate, God is Love,

The Father – The Son – The Holy Spirit

and He shows it to His creatures.

If you notice I did not say God knows how to love. The Bible says, "God is Love." That means, if it were possible to touch God you would be actually touching love. God's love is not how He feels. Love is the essence of His Being. Keep in mind that Lucifer has zero love and zero compassion. Even when God kills the creatures that He has made, He kills them because he loves them. Only God can do this; don't you ever try to kill anybody because you love him or her so much. Some people think that God is too loving to kill anyone.

I Samuel 2:6 tells us that he made and He also kills. Joshua 10:11 tells us that a couple kings got to gather and went up against Joshua and the children of Israel and God threw rocks at them from heaven and killed all of them. There is something about sin that you and I do not understand. When mankind crosses over the line of demarcation God has to stop it for its own good and the good of the universe. Man was made in the image of God in that he has the ability to love and show compassion. He has the ability to love God and his fellow man.

Man was made in the image of God in respect to certain spiritual faculties, which are an image or likeness of what exists in the Maker Himself. God accepts worship and His creatures are made with a desire to give worship to their Maker. Within our spiritual faculties, there is a built-in timekeeper that tells us there is a need and it is time to worship. Man is God's representative on the earth. He resembled his Creator with regard to his intellect, his moral qualities, his spiritual faculties, his love and affection, and his ability to rule over the earth, just

Travelling Through Rough Waters

to mention a few. It is our entire selves that reflect the image of God.

Jesus Has the Same Attributes as God the Father

Jesus Is Omnipotent (Matt. 28:18).
Jesus is all powerful. Jesus had the power to raise Himself up from the grave (John 2:19). Jesus answered, "Destroy this temple, and in three days I will rebuild it." Jesus was referring to His death when He made this statement.

Jesus Is Omniscient (1 Cor. 1:24).
Jesus has the wisdom of God the Father. Jesus knows everything. When Christ was on earth, He limited Himself only to know what the Father told Him. "From the beginning, the Word of God was there. The Word stood by the side of God, and the Word was fully God. There never was a time when the Word of God was not with God" (John. 1.2). Please note here that the second person of the Godhead is called, "The Word." God can call Himself anything He wants to.

Jesus Is Omnipresent (Matt. 28:18, 18:20).
Jesus is everywhere through the agency of the Holy Spirit. Wherever we preach the gospel, Jesus is there through the agency of the Holy Spirit. Again, this is a choice Jesus made. Jesus chose to limit Himself with the human body and continues to serve as our lawyer in heaven before the great tribunal.

The Father – The Son – The Holy Spirit

Jesus Is Immutable or Unchangeable.
Jesus is the same, He does not change. This change is referring to His character and nature.

Jesus's Name Testified to the Fact That He Is God
ELAH (Isa. 9:6): The Wonderful Counselor
EL-ELYON (Isa. 9:6): The Mighty God
EL-OLAM (Isa. 9:6): The Everlasting Father, and the Prince of Peace.
JESUS (Matt. 1:21): He shall save His people
EMMANUEL (Matt. 1:23): He is God with us.
CHRIST THE SON OF GOD (Matt. 16:16): Christ and God has the same substance

Jesus's Word Testifies that He Is God
Jesus gives eternal life (John 17:2). Only God can give eternal life. Jesus sends the Holy Spirit (John 14:16,26). Only God can give God a command.

Jesus Accepts Worship
The Disciples worship Him (Matt. 14:33).
Worship belongs only to God (Matt. 28:9).
The Canaanite woman worships Him (Matt. 15:24-25).
Every knee shall bow before Him (Phil. 2:10).

The Holy Spirit
The Holy Spirit is the third person of the Godhead.
The Holy Spirit is a Comforter (John 14:16).
The Holy Spirit is taking care of unfinished business in this world until Christ returns.

Travelling Through Rough Waters

The Holy Spirit helps us understand the Word of God, and when we forget God's Word, He will bring it back to our mind (John 14:26). The Holy Spirit is a person. The masculine gender "He" is attached to His name. So from our understanding of the Word of God, God the Father is a person. God the Son is a person. God the Holy Spirit is a person. (In heaven, there is no feminine gender, only masculine gender and please don't ask me why, ladies, because I do not know why. We shall be like the angels; they are neither men nor women as we understand it down here.) All three persons of the Godhead were together at creation. The Bible tells us that they all agreed to make mankind in the likeness of themselves (Gen. 1:26). The Godhead is one in mind and purpose. They are united in accomplishing one objective. This reality is demonstrated in the union of a husband and a wife. Two persons become one, not in body, but in mind and purpose.

Threefold Blessing from the Godhead
The Lord bless you and keep you.—God the Father

The Lord makes his face to shine on thee and be gracious unto thee.-God the Son.

The Lord lifts up His countenance upon thee and gives you peace.—God the Holy Spirit (Num. 6:24-26).

Chapter 15

Before the evil days come

Ecclesiastes 12:1-10 says that Solomon made a universal appeal to the youth. Not only to the youth of the Christian faith, but to the youth of the world as well. This chapter was written by three of the youths in my church. I wanted to get their perspective on the subject, so I asked my daughter, my grandson, and one other youth in church to address this subject for me. The following is a copy from the manuscript they had presented.

Travelling Through Rough Waters

My Daughter:

We are living in the close of earth's history and the youth of God's church are called upon to do something special for other youth who may not have a relationship with God. First of all, we the youth should consider it a privilege to be used by God. I asked these men behind me to let me be the second person to speak, realizing that I am a girl and I was hoping to learn something from them, but they pled the Fifth Amendment and as you can see I was outvoted. However, I am asking you for your undivided attention for the next ten or twelve minutes as I speak to you. I am looking at Ecclesiastes 12:1-5, and I would like to make three observations from this passage of scripture. First of all I shall look at the word "remember"; secondly I shall look at time as it relates to the youth; and finally, how quickly our desires change.

Remember

The word "remember" reminds us of something we have heard before. Before the class is dismissed, the teacher reminds us to remember that the homework is due tomorrow. This statement from the teacher reminds us that she has spoken to us before about something that was important and she is now reminding us about what she spoke about. The word remember reminds me of the wise man Solomon. Proverbs 3:2-3: My son or my daughter, don't forget what I told you. I told you to take my commandments seriously. If you do, you will live a long and happy life, and you will be successful in all that you do. To remember to do your homework will stop you from trying to get your report card out of the mail before your parents get to it. I guess all of us would say that remembering is important. Remembering keeps us from worrying or getting stressed. Remembering will keep many of us youth from getting into trouble with our parents and teachers. Some of us always get into trouble because we keep on forgetting. And that is why the Lord reminds us to remember him before it is too late. To get in trouble with our mothers or teachers is one thing, but it's a whole lot worse to get in trouble with the Lord.

Let me tell you a story about a lady; as a matter a fact, she was Lot's wife. The Lord went down to Sodom and Gomorrah and as you know the city was wicked. The Lord told Lot's wife to get out of the city and he told her not to look back. Everybody else remembered not to look back, but Lot's wife forgot all about what God had told her; she turned around and looked and she became a pillar of salt. Remembering the Lord when we are young will allow us to live long on the earth and finally live with Jesus in the earth made new, so the word "remember" is a word to remember.

Time as It Relates to the Youth

The years pass so quickly. I remember when my mother first brought me to this church. I was about nine years old. We were Catholic and I had my first communion, and it seemed as if it was the greatest thing in the world. Today I am a Seventh-day Adventist, and I am learning a new a perspective on life. From a born-again Catholic to a Seventh-day Adventist youth preacher, many of us may say, "I have time to be a good Christian, I do not need to

Travelling Through Rough Waters

rush," but a relationship with God can be developed by the old as well as the young. It is not something we add on as we go along the way; it is something we take with us.

Lillian Baxter wrote the song lyrics, "Take the name of Jesus with you, child of sorrow and of woe, it will joy and comfort give you, take it, then, wherever you may go." Isaiah started out his ministry at a very young age, so I ask if he was called at such a young age, then what makes you and I think that some of us sitting here in the congregation won't be called upon by God? The Bible says, "Seek the Lord while he may be found. Call upon Him while he is near." Florida has one of the largest populations of pediatric home care patients. What this tells me is, you do not have to be old before the evil days come. There are so many babies and young people who are having problems. We are going down faster than the older adults. Therefore, seek God while you can so that you can be a part of his work. The message is clear: we do not have time, we are dying before we get old. I challenge you, my fellow youth members; let us show our parents, the older adults, the church, and the community at large the power of God at work in us.

Desires and Feelings Change as We Grow Older

How quickly life changes, how quickly we see things differently. I heard about a worm called the caterpillar; today you see a little worm crawling on a blade of grass and a few weeks later you can see a butterfly flying in the air. As we get older in life, our thoughts change, our

Before the evil days come

ideas change, our whole perspective on life changes. I would like to say something to the adult and maybe to our parents. Don't be too hard on us. We will change like the caterpillar that turns into a beautiful butterfly; someday we will turn into a beautiful spiritual butterfly. Be patient with us, and your heart will be made glad.

Let me speak just for a few minutes to my friends and age group. Life changes; what we focus on today, tomorrow it will disappear. Things that seem so important to us today, tomorrow these things will have no value. Only one thing is guaranteed in life and that is our relationship with God; therefore, Jesus tells us to be serious about our relationship with Him. If you don't remember anything else I said today, please remember this, "Whatsoever we feed the mind with it will grow to like it, so if we only feed our minds on the things of the world, it will only like the things of the world, and that is the reason why Solomon said, 'Remember the Lord, when we are young, when we are feeding our minds with the things of the world before we get to a point of no return.'"

Youth, we are not the first to be called upon and asked to be faithful to our God. I can name you a few who were called upon and were faithful to the end: Samuel was about eight years old when he heard the voice of God calling his name in the middle of the night, and he answered, "Here I am, Lord, send me." He followed the Lord from the age of eight years old until he died at his home in Ramah. Shadrach, Meshach, and Abednego were between the ages of sixteen and eighteen when they were taken from Jerusalem to Babylon and they stood

Travelling Through Rough Waters

firm for God and never looked back.

   Queen Esther was a young lady when she was told by her uncle Mordecai to enter the beauty pageant of the Medo-Persian government. She eventually became the queen of the Medo-Persian emperor and she was faithful to the Lord. Naamen had a slave girl; she was a slave, but she was a Christian slave. She told her mistress, I wish to God that my master knew the God of Israel. He would just touch him and he would be made whole. Remember the Lord because the time is short, the evil days are upon us, and things change as we grow older.

My Grandson:
I would like to look at some of the changes that take place in our lives as we grow older and the reasons we should remember the Lord while we are young. I will discuss with you the following: Our senses will be affected by our age, romance will gradually fade, and our body will finally decay and return to the dust. Please remember that the evil days can come at age sixteen, or at age twenty. I have seen many who were seeing the evil days at age fifteen.

Our Five Senses Will Be Affected by the Evil Days
The Bible says, the youth should remember the Lord before the evil days come. Part of the evil days is to lose the five major senses. Based on the text, part of the problem the youth will face if they live long enough is their sense of sight will be dim or completely blind, and they will lose a good portion of their sense of feeling.

Before the evil days come

Many will lose to a great degree their sense of smell. Some may not enjoy their meals because they will lose their sense of taste. Many will not enjoy conversation with their family because their sense of hearing will be affected by old age, or premature old age.

The nerves that carry stimuli from the eye to the brain may stop working. The nerves that carry stimuli to the brain for the sense of touch may stop working. The nerves that carry stimuli to the brain with the sense of smell may stop working. The nerves that carry stimuli to the brain with the sense of taste may stop working. The nerves that carry stimuli to the brain with the sense of hearing may stop working. Just ask my grandfather; he will tell you that his mother always asked him to string the needle because she could not see. She always asked him to speak louder because she could not hear. She always told him that she did not want the food because it did not taste good. The evil days were upon her.

The elderly are not the only ones who are experiencing evil days; just ask my mother. She is a nurse and she will tell you that she has taken care of children and youth who could not feel anything below the waist, some who could not smell, and some who could not hear. The evil days are coming. The Lord wants us to give him our heart now, because most people who cannot see don't enjoy worship as well. Most people who cannot feel and smell don't even go to church. Most people who cannot taste and hear don't enjoy going to church. Therefore, God said come before the evil days get to you.

Travelling Through Rough Waters

Romance Will Gradually Fade

The Bible says, "The silver chain that holds us to our loved ones will break" (Eccles. 12:6). There will be no more romance, no more dating, no more marriages. You will be afraid to climb up to high places, your hair will turn white as the blossoms of the almond tree, and you will drag yourself along and rest after each step like an old grasshopper resting after each hop. You will not be able to come to church, because you are sick and you have no pleasure in loud noises like the guitar and drumbeats. You will have no pleasure in God, because as the previous speaker said, "Our mind gets to like what we feed into it and dislike everything else." The fact that when we were young we did not feed upon God, we will have no pleasure for God when the evil days come. Therefore, the Lord said, come to me before the evil days come to you.

Our Body Will Decay and Return to the Dust

Finally, our body will decay and return to the dust. Whatever we do, we must remember that we shall surely die. I appeal to you today, my fellow youth. Let us show to the world that we can be like Christ; let us tell it to our schools, our churches, and everywhere we go that we don't have to be like everybody else. We can be a little Daniel, We can be a little Shadrach, We can be a little Meshach, and We can be a little Abednego right where we are. My fellow youth, let us remember the Lord before the evil days come.

Before the evil days come

Speaker Number Three:
You have heard from the previous speakers that time is relative as it relates to the youth, our desires will change as we grow older, our eyesight will grow dim, we will hop around like the grasshopper resting after each hop. We will have no desire for food because our spiritual taste buds will lose their ability to taste...our body will finally decay and return to dust. I search diligently to find the right words to say, after hearing such mind-bothering words from the previous speakers. I conclude that we should be careful, not allowing our minds to be absorbed in the things of the world that are not eternally helpful, and we should fear God, and keep His commandment, for this is our duty.

Be Careful
We have heard the sum total of the whole matter. Life is not as carefree as some think it to be; therefore, we should be careful and make thoughtful decisions as we journey through life. We should enjoy our lives, but we should never forget that the evil days are coming. We should not let the evil days lay hands on us unprepared. In response to the evil days, the songwriter penned these words, "We will watch and we will pray, with lamps trim and burning, the evil days will come to all others like a thief in the night, but we know that she is near, but we know not the day, as spring shows that summer is not far away. Hold fast till I come, sweet promise is given, the kingdom is restored, to you it shall be given, come enter my joy, sit down on my throne, bright crowns are in waiting, hold fast till I come."

Travelling Through Rough Waters

We should be careful of the friends we keep. We should be careful of the places we go. We should be careful of the things we see. We should be careful of the music we listen to. We should be careful of the way we dress. We should be careful of the people we fall in love with, because the evil days are coming. David said, the Lord is my shepherd and I shall not want. David said, the shepherd will let us lie down in green pastures, beside the still waters and he will restore our life. Only when we follow the good shepherd are we led to green pastures beside the still waters. Even if I have to walk through the valley of the shadow of death I will fear no evil, because the Good shepherd will be with me.

Death casts a frightening shadow over us, because we are entirely helpless in its presence. We can struggle with other enemies, such as pain, suffering, injury, and disease, but strength and courage cannot overcome death. Death has the final word. Only one person can walk with us through death's dark valley and bring us safely to the other side and David said He is the Good Shepherd. We should follow the Good Shepherd, because life is uncertain and the Good Shepherd will take good care of us. He will take us beside the still waters, He will restore our soul, and then He will give us eternal life.

Fear God

Because the evil days are coming, we are asked to fear God. To fear God does not mean to be afraid of Him, it means to reverence God. It conveys the thought of absolute loyalty to God, fully surrendering to His will.

Before the evil days come

We are asked to fear God today because other young people are worshiping gods of materialism, and gods of pleasure. You and I are called today to give our absolute loyalty to our God.

God would never have called us to do something that He knows we could not do, so let us buckle up our shoes and take up the task before us. Some of us may say today, I am too young to fear God, I am too young to give God total loyalty. I need some time to enjoy life. I need some time to enjoy a little more pleasure before I fear God. The Bible says, If you hear my voice, harden not your heart. There is a way that seems right to a young person, but the end thereof are the ways of death. Some of us sit and we listen, but we do not plan to change.

I heard a story about a young man who had been stealing lumber from the place he was working. The young man could not deal with his nagging conscience anymore so he decided to go to confession. In confession to the priest he admitted that for years he had been stealing building supplies from the lumberyard where he worked. "What did you take?" his parish priest asked. I took enough lumber to build my own home and enough to build a cottage by the lake. "This is very serious," The priest said. "I shall have to think of a far-reaching penance. Have you ever done a retreat?" No, Father, the young man replied, but if you can get architect to draw the plan, I can get the lumber. Some people do not plan to change, but the call is loud and clear today. "Fear God, surrender completely to him because the evil days are coming.

Travelling Through Rough Waters

Keep His Commandment

My final point is keeping God's commandment. What to do with the evil days? Keep God's commandment. Keeping God's commandment is our duty. Commandment-keeping youth don't worry themselves about the evil days. Shadrach, Meshach, and Abednego were commandment-keeping youth. When Nebuchadnezzar, the king of Babylon, requested of them to break the second commandment and dishonor the God of heaven, the young men said, "O King, with due respect, we cannot bow down and worship another god, we have to obey God's word." The king got upset. Those boys knew it was dangerous to make the king upset, but they were commandment-keeping youth. They knew that their evil days were just around the Connor, but they were commandment-keeping youth. They knew that ye that dwelleth in the secret place of the Most High will abide under the shadow of the Almighty. The king called up homeland security and devised a plan to bring about premature evil days for the boys, but David said, the Lord is my Shepherd, I shall not want, He will lead me beside the still waters, and He will restore my soul, and give me eternal life. We talk the talk, but we must be ready to walk the walk. Sometimes evil days may come and we are not ready for them, but we must say like Daniel, when he was about to be put into the lion's den: My God is able to deliver me.

When Nebuchadnezzar called up homeland security, God the Father called up universal security. Nebchadnezzar had his plan, but God the Father also had His plan. Nebuchadnezzar planned to burn those boys, but God the Father planned to save those boys.

Before the evil days come

Nebuchadnezar told his men to throw the boys into the fire and God the Father told Jesus to take the heat out of the fire. There are evil days coming, my fellow youth. Let us get ourselves together before it comes.

Chapter 16

Who Changed It?

Some people go to church on Sunday, some people go to church on Saturday, and some people tell me that there is nothing wrong with worshiping God on either days because it doesn't matter to God which day we worship Him. After the Flood, God called Abraham and from Abraham the Jewish nation evolved. History tells us that the Jews worship God on the seventh day or Sabbath. God told the Jewish people to worship Him on the seventh day (Exod. 20:8-11). Christianity evolved from Judaism, so why did we change from worshiping

Who Changed It?

God on the day He told the Jewish people to worship Him? And who was the one who changed the day of worship? One of the reasons I love the job of a "Biblical Reporter" is that I have the ability to dig and find answers to my reader's questions. Now, my next assignment is to find out who changed the day of worship and how God feels about the change.

Do we get to choose the day when we worship God, or does God choose which day we worship Him? I know that people worship God every day, but this is not where I am going. Let me try to explain what I am saying by using two lovers' relationship. Most people who are in love try to talk on the phone as much as possible. Some of us speak many times a day on the phone, but a phone conversation is nothing in comparison to an actual date to meet with each other face-to-face. All lovers look forward to this face-to-face interaction. Well, worshiping God every day is like the day-to-day phone conversation, but on Sunday or Saturday and for some of us Friday would be the face-to-face meeting or interaction. So now I can get back to my point. Who changed the time God sets to meet with mankind for worship?

It should be noted also that the Jews were not even the first people God told to worship Him on Sabbath (Saturday). When God made mankind, He set an example for us to worship Him on Saturday. This is what it says, "Thus the heavens and the earth was finished, and all the host of them, and on the seventh day God ended His work which He had made, and He rested on the seventh day from all his work which He had made. And God blessed the seventh day and sanctified it, because

Travelling Through Rough Waters

that in it He had rested from all His work which God created and made" (Gen. 2:1-3). II Timothy 2:15 tells us, "Study to show ourselves approved unto God, a workman that need not to be ashamed, rightly dividing the word of truth." According to this text, God wanted us to study His word, and be not afraid to explain or present correctly the message in God's word with tact and conviction. So based on this charge, let us go and look at the Word of God to find out who the Bible predicts would change the day of worship and did it really happen.

Daniel is a prophet. You may call him the biblical historian and predictor of the future, so between Daniel and John the Revelator we will find this person who changed the day of worship. So let us start with Daniel. Daniel 7:1-4 tells us,

It was during the first year of Nebuchadnezzar's grandson, Belshazzer, that the Lord gave me visions and dreams. He asked me to write them down. This is what I saw, the first vision came while I was lying in my bed. I saw an ocean being whipped up by mighty winds coming from all directions. Then four huge animals came up out of the stormy sea, one after another, each one different. The first animal looked like a lion, but it had huge wings that looked like those of an eagle. As I was looking I saw the wings torn off and it was made to stand up like a man and a human heart was given to it so it stopped acting like a lion, then it disappeared. (*Clear Word Bible*)

Daniel 7:5 tells us about a second animal: "The second animal that came up out of the angry waves looked like a bear. As it stood, it raised up one side more than the other. I notice that it had three ribs in its mouth and

Who Changed It?

someone told it to go ahead and devour as much meat as it wanted, then it disappeared."

Daniel 7:6 tells us about a third animal coming out of the angry waves that looked like a leopard, but it had four heads. It also had four huge wings like those of a large bird. It was very strong and nothing could stand in its way as it reached across the earth, then it too disappeared.

Daniel 7:7-9 tell us about a fourth and final beast in Daniel's vision: "As I looked I saw the fourth animal coming out of the boisterous waves. It was a huge animal and looked like nothing I had ever seen before, it was powerful and extremely frightening to look at. It had huge iron teeth and chewed up everything it killed and what was left, it trampled down with its huge feet. It had ten horns coming out of the top of its head." Daniel said as he was looking at the ten horns he saw a little horn pushing its way up in the middle of these ten horns, and it pushed three of the previous horns out of the way to make room for itself. As he closely watched, he noticed that this little horn had human eyes and a mouth full of pride and arrogance, and before the animal disappeared the scene changed and he saw thrones were been set up for a special occasion in heaven (*Clear Word Bible*).

We are looking for who changed the day of worship, so why are we discussing animals? What do these animals represent? Well, Daniel will tell us. In Daniel 7:17: "The four animals that you saw coming up out of the stormy sea represent four kingdoms which will arise one after another." Remember in biblical prophecy, seas represent people (Rev. 17:15). Wind represents war (Jer.

Travelling Through Rough Waters

49:36-37). And beasts represent kingdoms (Dan. 7:17). If the animals represent kingdoms, then these four animals that Daniel saw in his vision would represent the four world powers in the past. The first animal would be Babylon, which ruled the world from 605–539 BC. The second animal would be Medo-Persia, which ruled the world from 539–331 BC. The third animal would be Greece, which ruled the world from 331–168 BC, and the fourth and final animal would be Rome, which ruled the world from 168 BC to 476 AD.

I don't know if you are noticing, but for me to find who changed the day of worship I have to go way back in time; but as a certain pastor used to tell his members when he was preaching, "Bear with me, I am going somewhere," so I am asking you to bear with me. I promise you we will find out who made the change. If you remember in Daniel 7:8, when we were looking at Daniel's vision with the fourth animal, this animal had ten horns and Daniel said he noticed another little horn was pushing its way up and in the process of pushing it got rid of three of the previous horns to make way for itself. Daniel said that this little horn had human eyes and a mouth speaking great things, boastful and arrogant things.

By now you should know that these horns that we are discussing are not the real horns of an animal. According to Daniel, these horns are kingdoms with a human being leading out (Dan. 7:24). So what is this little kingdom or person who is moving up the ranks in the Roman kingdom? Daniel said this little horn is diverse from the other horns (Dan. 7:24). What does he mean by diverse? Well everybody knows that to be diverse is to be different,

Who Changed It?

but in what way is this little horn different from the rest? I think that we are on to something. Could it be that this little horn has something to do with our subject? Let us keep searching.

Listen to this statement, speaking of the little horn, "Out of the ruins of the Roman Empire, there gradually arose a new order of states whose central point was the Papal See, therefore, inevitable, resulted a position not only new, but very different from the former" (*The Church and Churches*, 42-43). History tells us that out of the ruins of the Roman empire there arose a new position that was not only new but different. Do you remember this word, "Different," from Daniel? Remember that the fourth animal was the Roman Empire and Daniel said the little horn that pushed itself to a comfortable position was different from all the other horns.

Now history tells us that the little horn that was different in Daniel 7:24 is the Papal See. Let us read it again, "Out of the ruins of the Roman Empire, there gradually arose a new order of states whose central point was the Papal See, therefore, inevitable, resulted a position not only new, but very different from the former." Now we can start focusing on some differences that Daniel mentions. Based on what we read from *The Church and Churches*, we conclude this, the fourth animal is the Roman Empire, and the horns represent smaller kingdoms that would rule in the same territory. All of these horns are politically motivated. They have not one religious nerve in their political body, but history tells that the little horn is a religious power, not a political power. From the pages of history, we notice that this little horn

Travelling Through Rough Waters

is the Papal See, which is a religious entity, so you can see where Daniel is coming from when he said the little horn is different. Everybody else is looking for political power, but the little horn is looking for religious power.

Now, let us go straight to our punch line. Daniel is still speaking about this little horn, which by now we know that Daniel is talking about the Papacy. This is what Daniel said about the little horn (or you may say, this is what Daniel said about the Papacy) in Daniel 24-25 "This little horn will try to take the place of God on earth and will actually boast about it. It will wage an aggressive campaign against God's people and will think to change God's law" (Clear Word Bible). It should be noted that the day of worship is a law that God gave to his people. In Exodus 20:8-11 we read, "Remember the Sabbath day to keep it holy. Six days he shall do labor and do all thy work, but the seventh day is the Sabbath of the Lord thy God. In it thou shall do no work, thou nor thy son, nor thy daughter, nor thy manservant, nor thy maidservant, nor thy cattle, nor thy strangers that is within thy gates, for in six days the Lord made heaven and earth, the sea and all that in them is, and rested the seventh day, wherefore, the Lord blessed the Sabbath day and hollowed it." Listen to this statement from *Ancient Church*: "In the interval between the days of the Apostles and the conversion of Constantine....Rites and ceremonies of which neither Paul or Peter ever heard crept silent into use and then claimed the ranks of divine institution" (*Ancient Church*, vi, vii).

Daniel predicted the change of God's law and the church admits it. the question we started out with, was,

Who Changed It?

"Who changed the day of worship?" and here is the answer: "The church...after changing the day of rest from the Jewish Sabbath or the seventh day of the week to the first, made the third commandment refer to Sunday as the day to be kept holy as the Lord's Day" (*Catholic Encyclopedias*, Vol. 4, 153).

"You may read the Bible from Genesis to Revelation and you will not find a single line authorizing the sanctification of Sunday. The scripture enforces the religious observance of Saturday" (*The Faith of Our Fathers*, 89).

From the Convert Catechism:
Question: Which is the Sabbath Day?
Answer: Saturday is the Sabbath day.
Question: Why do we observe Sunday instead of Saturday?
Answer: We observe Sunday instead of Saturday because the Catholic Church transferred solemnity from Saturday to Sunday. (Peter Giereman, *1948*, 50)

So the little horn changed the day of worship from Saturday to Sunday. God tells us to remember the Sabbath (Saturday) day to keep it holy, and the Catholic Church tells us to keep holy the first day of the week or Sunday, so who are you going to obey? The church or God?

"Reverend Philip Carrington, Anglican Archbishop of Quebec, sent local clergymen into a huddle today by saying outright that there was nothing to support Sunday being kept holy. Carrington definitely told a church meeting in the city of straight-laced Protestantism that

Travelling Through Rough Waters

tradition, not the Bible, had made Sunday the day of worship." (*Toronto Daily Star*, Oct. 26, 1949)

"Sabbath....A Hebrew word signifying rest....Sunday was a name given by the heathens to the first day of the week, because it was the day on which they worshipped the sun." (John Eadie, DD., LL,D. *A Bible Cyclopedia*, 561)

The first Sunday law in 321, "On the venerable day of the sun, let the magistrates and people residing in the cities rest, and let all workshops be closed." (Edict of Constantine, AD 321)

"Christians shall not Judaize (Keep Sabbath) and be idle on Saturday (Sabbath Original) but shall work on that day, but the Lord's Day they shall especially honor." (*Council of Laodicea*, Canon 29)

"Sunday is founded not on scripture, but on tradition and is distinctly a Catholic institution." (*Catholic Record*, Sept. 17, 1893)

"The authority of the Church could therefore not be bound to the authority of the scripture, because the Church had changed...the Sabbath into Sunday not by command of Christ, but by its own authority." (*Canon and Tradition*, 263)

Jesus said, "These people honor me with their lips, but their hearts are far from Me. They worship in vain, their teachings are but rules taught by man....You have a fine way of setting aside the commands of God in order to observe your own traditions" (Mark 7:7-9) "If you love me keep my commandment." (John 14:15)

Come with me and I will show you what all the heads of all your local church leaders

Who Changed It?

are saying:

The Churches Comment on the Change of the Sabbath

The Baptist
"There was and is a commandment to keep holy the Sabbath day, but that Sabbath day was not Sunday…it will be said, however, and with some show of triumph, that the Sabbath was transferred from the seventh to the first day of the week….Where can the record of such a transaction be found? Not in the New Testament, absolutely not. There is no scriptural evidence of the change of the Sabbath institution from the seventh to the first day of the week."
(Dr. Edward T. Hiscox, *The Baptist Manual*)

The Catholic
"You may read the Bible from Genesis to Revelation, and you will not find a single line authorizing the sanctification of Sunday. The Scriptures enforce the religious observance of Saturday, a day which we (Catholics) never sanctify." (James Cardinal Gibbons, *The Faith of Our Fathers*, 111)

Christian
"There never was any change of the Sabbath from Saturday to Sunday. There is not in any place in the Bible any intimation of such a change." (*First Day Observance*, 17-19)

Church of Christ

Travelling Through Rough Waters

"I do not believe that the Lord's Day came in the room of the Jewish Sabbath, or that the Sabbath was changed from the seventh to the first day." (Alexander Campbell, (*Washington Report* October 8, 1921)

Methodist
"Take the matter of Sunday....there is no passage telling Christians to keep that day, or to transfer the Jewish Sabbath to that day." (Harris Franklin Rall, *Christian Advocate*, July 2, 1942)

Lutheran
"The observance of the Lord's day (Sunday) is founded not on any command of God, but on the authority of the church." (Augsburg Confession of Faith, quoted in *Catholic Sabbath Manual*, part 2 Chapter 1, Section 10)

Presbyterian
"The Christian Sabbath (Sunday) is not in the scripture, and was not by the primitive church called by the Sabbath." (Dwight, *Theology*, Vol. 4, 401)

"The notion of a formal substitution by apostolic authority of the Lord's day (meaning Sunday) for the Jewish Sabbath (or the first for the seventh day)...and the transference to it, perhaps in a spiritualized form, of the sabbatical obligation established by the promulgation of the Forth Commandment, has no basis whatsoever either in Holy Scripture or in Christian antiquity." (Sir William Smith & Samuel Cheetham, *A Dictionary of Christian Antiquities*, Vol. 2, 182)

Encyclopedia

Who Changed It?

"It must be confessed that there is no law in the New Testament concerning the first day." (McLintock and Strong, *Cyclopedia of Biblical, Theological and Ecclesiastical Literature*, Vol. 9, 196)

Though many individual pastors may argue the point, we have not found one single Sunday-Keeping organization yet, which did not in its official literature plainly admit that there is no scripture to support Sunday observance.

We started out with the question, "Who changed the day of worship that God commanded Adam and Eve, our first parents, to worship Him, and He called attention to the day of worship again on Mount Zion to Moses and the children of Israel to remember to keep the seventh day Holy. I have taken you with me and you have seen for yourself that Daniel predicted that the little horn of Daniel 7:24-25 would change God's law and I have shown to you that keeping the Sabbath day holy is a part of God's law. I also showed to you that Daniel predicted the change and history confirmed the prophet's prediction. History pinpointed for us who the little horn is (the Papal See, or the papacy). The Catholic Church finally testified to the fact that they changed God's holy Sabbath day and commanded all mankind to keep Sunday the first day of the week instead.

The question to the Catholic Church was, "Which day is the Sabbath Day? **Answer:** Saturday is the Sabbath day. Question: Why do we observe Sunday instead of Saturday? **Answer:** We observe Sunday instead of Saturday because the Catholic Church transferred solemnity from Saturday to Sunday" (Peter Giereman,

Travelling Through Rough Waters

1948, 50). "You may read the Bible from Genesis to Revelation, and you will not find a single line authorizing the sanctification of Sunday. The Scriptures enforce the religious observance of Saturday, a day which we (Catholics) never sanctify" (James Cardinal Gibbons, *The Faith of Our Fathers*, 111).

As a reporter I have finished my job. One reporter on Fox News used to say, "I report and you decide." So I have reported to you that the day God commanded us to worship Him is Sabbath (Saturday). Now you must decide whether you want to obey God or the Catholic Church.

Chapter 17

The Test

The world is a school and time is the teacher. If we live long enough, you and I will be tested by the teacher. How will you fare out? Will the result be excellent, fair, or poor? Every one of us will be tested. If you already had your midterm exam, the final is coming soon. When Christ was on earth He, too, had to take His test. Even though He made the world and He made time, He was tested by the things of the world. Jesus had three tests during His earthly life and he passed all of them. It is important to note that if we do not pass the tests of life we

Travelling Through Rough Waters

cannot be saved in God's kingdom. Jesus passed all three of His earthly tests and He is now standing on the right hand of His Father.

Let's look at the tests Jesus had to take. There were three of them; we will look at each separately. And we shall look at the events surrounding the time of the test. But before we look at each test separately, let us look at the passage of scriptures in Matthew 4:1-11. Immediately after Jesus was baptized, He went into the wilderness to pray and to prepare for His ministry. But the Devil would not leave Him alone. While in the wilderness, Jesus fasted for forty days, and He became extremely hungry. Then the Devil confronted Him by disguising himself as an angel from heaven. He told Jesus that His fast was over and that His Father had given Him permission to use divine power to turn some of the desert stones into bread. "If you are the Son of God, that should be no problem," Satan said. But as famished as Jesus was, He recognized who was tempting Him. So He answered, "The scripture teaches that man is not to put survival before obedience to God's word."

But the Devil didn't give up. Next, he picked Jesus up and carried Him to Jerusalem to the highest point on the temple wall, overlooking the valley below. Then he dared Jesus to jump to prove His faith in God. He even flattered Him for relying so firmly on God's word and quoted from the Old Testament scripture (Ps. 91:11), which says, "God will instruct His angels to watch over you and take care of you. When you fall, they will catch you." But Jesus knew that the Devil had twisted the scripture. So He answered him by quoting another Scripture (Exod.

17:2, Deut. 6:16): "You shall not test God's love by demanding that He demonstrate His care for you."

Still the Devil did not give up. Next he carried Christ to the top of a mountain, giving Him a panoramic view of the many luxuries available in the world and all the comforts that go with power and wealth. Then he turned to Jesus and said, "I'll give you all this, plus all the people in the world, if you will simply acknowledge that I gave it to you. Instantly Jesus responded to this offer of a life of ease by saying, "Get away from me, Satan, because the scripture says, 'Man shall acknowledge God as owner of this planet and worship and serve Him only.' Then the Devil left. By this time His strength was totally gone, and He lay there dying. But God sent an angel from heaven to revive Him and assure Him of His Father's approval and love."

Jesus just got baptized in the church and the Holy Spirit told Him to leave everybody and go into the wilderness to pray and fast for forty days. Many people think that the church is a place of peace. Once I have accepted Christ everything is going to be all right. But nobody told us that we think those thoughts in our mind. The first thing the Spirit directed Christ to do when He came into the church was to pray and fast. Now you can look at this in two ways: one, you can say, "The church can be a very uncomfortable place sometimes, I cannot even get myself situated before I've got to start fasting." Or you could say, "The Holy Spirit is getting me ready for the tedious task before me." The business of church cannot be put on the sideline until the end of the week when we go to church, because the church today

Travelling Through Rough Waters

becomes more complex than our everyday lives. There is this constant threat of you and I missing the mark when we are a member of the church. Jesus did not fuss about it; like a good member of the church He obeyed the voice of the Lord and went into the wilderness. I want you to watch Jesus as he prepared for his pop-test. In the physical school they call it pop-quiz, but this was not a quiz, it was a real test. I call the first test a pop-test, because Jesus did not know that it was coming for him. Pop-test or a pop-quiz is a test that is not expected. It catches the students off guard.

The record said the Devil showed up like an angel from heaven and lied to Jesus. The angel told Jesus that His Father had given him permission to make bread out of the stone. Isn't it good to know God and the way he does things? Jesus recognized the Devil right away. You see, while Jesus was fasting, he was studying God's word. If you stay with the Lord you can spot a liar from a mile away.

Here Is Test #1

The Devil who administered the test did not plan for Jesus to pass it. Jesus was extremely hungry after fasting for forty days and forty nights. The Devil showed up in the wilderness and took advantage of His physical needs and said, "Since you are God's Son, tell these stones to turn into loaves of bread." Let me say something about the test. Jesus had the power to turn the stones into loaves of bread. The Devil would not tell Jesus to do something he knows He could not do. Here is my punch line: When the Devil tempts you and me, he tempts us on something that we are able to do. Something that we have power and authority to do. Satan tempts us on things that are easy for us to do. He tempts us on those things that our body gravitates after. He tempts us on things that we have been wondering about, things that we have been thinking about as to what it would be like to do it. A few people you have been thinking of telling a few things.

Jesus, aren't you hungry? Make some bread. There is nothing like having some hot bread coming out of the oven when you are really hungry. Satan acts as if there is nothing to it, just do it. But it is a test, the test of life. If you fail the test of life, you and I cannot live with Jesus on the other side, because only those who pass the test shall be with Him. When Satan comes with his pop-test, it does not seem as if it is a test. Someone in the church just stepped over the line and I put him or her in his place. That was not a test, I just let her know where I stood, no big deal. Well it was a pop-test; it was a part of your grade and you just failed. You remember I told you that a pop-test is presented in such a way that you do not know when it is are coming, but if you keep on failing those tests you are going to flunk the course of life.

Jesus did not fail the pop-test. While he was fasting he was also praying and reading the Scroll, so when Satan came with the test, He said to him that in the book of Deuteronomy 8:3, God said that it takes more than bread to stay alive and mankind should not put physical survival before obedience to God's word. Sometimes our desires cry out for recognition. Sometimes our pride cries out for recognition. Sometimes justice cries out

Travelling Through Rough Waters

for recognition. Sometimes our desires dominate our rational capability, but we must remember one thing: Life is more than just physical satisfaction. Life is more than just making sure that I get my fair share. Life is more than just making sure that nobody takes advantage of me. Life is a test and we must pass the test. Never should we put physical survival before obedience to God's word. So the first test was a test for the appetite or the desire. Can we resist our desires? Some people say if it feels good do it, how can something be so wrong? But Satan only tests us on things that feel good, things that taste good, and things that make us look good.

Here Is Test #2
The Devil did not give up when he found out that Jesus was a better scholar than he thought. He decided to do something drastic this time because Jesus was no pushover. He went back to Jesus and assaulted Him; he did not even ask permission to touch the person of Christ, he just grabbed Him and picked Him up bodily and carried Him to the highest point on top of the temple overlooking the city of Jerusalem and the valley below. When the Devil comes at you and me and he does not get his way, he gets mad and returns to us like a growling lion. Sometimes you see people behaving with you in a certain way and you have to wonder, what did I do? Why are you so upset with me? There are some situations you and I encounter in the church and you have to pull back into your corner and wonder, does this church provide a heaven for these kinds of people?

Well the answer is yes. Sometimes the church becomes

a center for every unclean bird, but don't you go anywhere, because God knows how to get rid of unclean birds out of the church. The Devil will use people in the church to do his dirty work, and some of us are just glad to be used by him as if it is a big thing to work for the Devil. He does not pay better than God. The Devil always pays minimum wage. If you plan to work for the Devil, you will live in a mess because he does not pay enough for you to survive. You can always count on Jesus to be in your corner. Jesus said, "Come unto me, all of you who labor and are heavy-laden and I will give you rest" (Matt. 11:28). In Isaiah He tells us, I will give power to those who are faint and to them who have no might and whom other people look down upon, I will increase their strength. I will renew their strength and they shall mount with wings as eagles, they shall run and never get weary (Isa. 40:28-31).

In administrating the second test the Devil did not come as an angel of light, because Jesus already found out who he was. So he put Jesus on top of the church and told him to jump. What are you worrying about, Jesus? Are you afraid? Remember what God said in Psalm 91: He will send angels to catch you when you jump, so you will not get hurt. Come on, Jesus, you do not have any faith in your Father, jump, you say He loves you, what are you worrying about? He does the same thing to us. When our plans fail, he puts it in our hearts to doubt God's love and care for us. There are so many people turning away from God today because they do not trust Him anymore. Satan tested them on their faith in God and they failed the test. Satan will put mountains

Travelling Through Rough Waters

in your way, then tell us that it is God's responsibility to remove those mountains. And if God chooses not to move those mountains, he tempts us to give up our faith in God. But the next time Satan comes to you about God, tell him that you do not serve God for what you can get out of Him; you serve God because you love Him. And in due time He will supply all my needs. The next time Satan comes, tell him that God is good all the time. He is good when He does things for me and He is good when he chooses not to do anything for me.

The second test had to do with faith in our heavenly Father to supply all our needs, and Jesus passed it with flying colors. Jesus told Satan, God's children should not test God's love and His power to protect them by asking Him to publicly demonstrate His care for them (Matt. 11:7). It is a sin to tell God to prove to us that He cares. We should believe that God cares and in time of need He will be there for us. Satan will tell you, you can give up your principles for once, because you might never get this opportunity again, and if you listen to him, you have just failed the pop-test. You should have done just what Jesus did, by quoting the scripture: "You shall not test God's love and His power to protect you by going against His word and asking Him to publicly demonstrate His care for you in spite of your disobedience." I have been tested many times, you have been tested many times to doubt God's care and guidance in our lives, but God has planted a seed in my heart and it has been growing. This seed is God's love for me and it has been growing over the years, and nobody can tell me that God does not love me.

It makes no difference how many trials He may allow me to go through, I believe in my heart that better days are coming for me. Just wait on the Lord and do not complain. He knows what He is doing and Mrs. White said that when it is all over I would prefer no other way. Sometimes I cannot see my way, but I believe that God is coming. Sometimes it seems as if I will not make it, but God is on His way. So the second test was to put doubt in Christ's mind about His Father's faithfulness toward Him. How about you today, do you question God sometimes? Watch out for that pop-test.

Here Is Test #3

The Devil administered his final test. He picked up Christ again and carried Him to a very high mountain and gave him a panoramic view of all the wealth in the world and all the comforts that goes with power and wealth. You think that running with Satan is something, but how would you feel having Satan carry you all over the place on his shoulder and you are pretty much aware of what he is doing? You ask God to deliver you and He has done nothing for you and Satan is doing whatever he wants to do with you. If it were not for God's mercy, Satan would do the same thing he did to Christ with us. We complain that our trials are hard to bear, but we need to give God thanks for His goodness toward us. Satan would like to take us sometimes to the George Washington Bridge in New York and read to us Psalm 91 and then tell us to jump. He might even try to push us off the bridge.

So Satan picked up Christ again and carried Him to the mountaintop and gave him a panoramic view of everything,

Travelling Through Rough Waters

then he turned to Jesus and said, "I'll give you all this, plus the people in the world if you will simply acknowledge that I gave it to you." Jesus responded, "Get away from me, Satan, because the scripture says man shall recognize God alone as owner of this planet and accept Him only as its ruler." The Devil got mad and left Jesus in the desert. That is how the Devil is, always getting mad with God's people when he cannot have his way. But I don't care if he gets mad; I just want to hold on to Jesus. By this time Christ was very weak, all vital signs of life were fading. It seemed as if He was going to die, then an angel from heaven came quickly and revived Him.

The angel let Him know that God the Father and the host of heaven have been watching the entire experience with him and the Devil, and God is well pleased with the stand he took. God is watching us too, every day as we take our test. He wants to say that he is well pleased with us. The third test had to do with who is the authority of our life. Satan asked Christ to give allegiance to him. Accept me as the authority of His life and I will give you everything this world has to offer. And Jesus said no to the Devil. If you notice every test that the Devil presented to Christ, he presented them at the weakest point of His life. When he tested Him with food, Jesus was very hungry; when he tested Him with questioning God's love for Him, Christ was at a point where he really needed to hear from God. When he tested Him with the wealth of this world, Christ was poor to the point that He could not even buy food to eat. Well, the Bible says He was hungry. Who have you ever heard had money in his pocket and died from hunger.

The Test

Jesus had no money, and that is why the Devil told him to worship him and he would give him wealth, which is money. But just look at how Christ responded to every one of the tests. He was dying for food; however, he told the Devil that He was not going to make any bread to save His life. His life was in God's hands. Let Him do as He pleases with me. When the Devil tested him about God's love for Him, He responded by saying, nowhere in the scripture does God teach His people to foolishly put their lives in danger, then ask God to prove his love by protecting them. Don't think for a moment that the Devil did not let Christ think that He was going to fall off the roof and die; but love for God conquers all fears. The Devil wanted to kill Christ, but he knew that he could not kill Him, so he told Christ, you kill yourself and Christ said to the Devil, no deal.

When the Devil tested Christ on the wealth of this world, Christ could have really done well with a few dinero we would call it a few dollars, but under no circumstances He was going to put his physical needs before the command of God. He would bear the hunger and obey His father; He would bear his pain on the pinnacle of the temple while defending the character of God. He was willing to suffer shame and disgrace, while testifying to the Devil that His Father was the ruler of this world. When the Devil left Him, the angel came and told Him that God has approved of how he conducted himself. Christianity is not about hunger, it is not about what God can do to protect us, it is not about wealth and power. It is a principle that God asked us to uphold. Can we uphold this principle?

Travelling Through Rough Waters

Can we pass the test today? Are you able? Our test is severe, it requires our blood, it requires everything in us that makes us a woman or a man. Are you willing to give yourself, can you resist the urge to sin? Every knee must bow and every tongue must confess. We all have our own test and Jesus showed us how to pass the test so we can come and live with the heavenly family. We are not the only ones who must be tested and tried. Revelation 6:9 John the Revelator said, I look and I saw an altar and under the altar there were dead men's bones, representing those who were killed for their faith. They cried out for justice, saying, Almighty God, how much longer do we have to wait? And the answer came back: You must wait for the rest of your brothers and sisters. They, too, must be tested and tried. They must pass their test and come out as pure gold.

We are living in the worst phase of earth's history. We are living at a time when the love of many is waxing cold. There is a form of godliness, but the people are denying the power of God; nevertheless, we must find strength from within and hold on to Jesus. We must pass our test, because our brothers and sisters who have gone on before us are waiting on us. We must be faithful, we must be true to God in our hearts; don't try to fake it because God knows our hearts. Will you pass you test of life today? May God help us to pass.

Chapter 18

Breaking free from the stronghold of my past

"Do not think about what I have done in the past, do not focus on what happened then, watch out for the new thing I am going to do, it already started, can you see it? I will make a road through your wilderness and I will create many rivers in your desert land" (Isa. 43:18-19). These were the words of Isaiah to the people of Israel. I heard a story about a little dog that had been kept on a twenty-foot leash for years, tied to a tree. The

Travelling Through Rough Waters

owner came out and fed him and played with him occasionally, but the dog remained on the leash. When this little dog saw other dogs passing by, he would run right to the end of the leash and then the leash would pull him back. After a while, he knew exactly how far to go even though he wanted to chase the other dogs, so he would run to the end of the leash and stop. By now the dog had calculated in his mind the distance he could go. There was a psychological leash that now controlled his behavior.

The physical leash did not have to drag him back anymore; his psychological leash would tell him just how far he could go. One day the owner felt sorry for the dog and decided to let him loose for a little while. The owner thought the dog would take off running. Another dog came by and just like before this little dog took off running at the other dog. But to the owner's surprise, when the little dog got to the place where the leash would usually jerk him back, he stopped and did not go any further. The dog was free, but he just did not realize it.

Many of us have been doing the same thing this little dog did and we will be doing the same thing for a long time, but God said He is going to do a new thing in your life. God said to the people of Israel, Do not think about the past. Do not allow it to come into your mind. Now, at first glance at the passage we welcome such an idea because we want to get rid of a lot of things in our past. Many of us have painful pasts that have left psychological scars, so the idea of leaving the past behind is a welcome thought. Certainly, I do not believe that the children of Israel would mind leaving behind their experience of

Breaking free from the stronghold of my past

slavery as they headed for the future. I do not think that they would mind leaving behind the bloody marks of the whip on their backs in slavery. Many of us wouldn't mind leaving behind days of poverty.

But leaving the past behind is easier said than done for many of us, because we live our lives backward instead of forward. It is very hard to do things backward, but mentally we are just the opposite. Many of us think better backward than forward. We know what happened yesterday, but we can only guess or imagine about tomorrow, thus it always seems easier to live in the past. God has loosened our chains of depression, our chains of addictions, our chains of personal defeats, our chains of bad attitudes, our chains of fear. The problem is, we are still controlled by our psychological chains. But God's words to us today comes from Isaiah, "Do not think about what I have done in the past, do not focus on what happened then, watch out for the new thing I am going to do, it already started, can you see it? I will make a road through your wilderness and I will create many rivers in your desert land" (Isa. 43:18-19).

Such welcome news, a road through my wilderness and rivers in my desert, but I wonder if it is true. Of all the troubles I had last year, I don't know. This is what I am talking about, always thinking backward. Isaiah tells us not to allow the past to come to remembrance. I am going to do a new thing for you. This new thing that God is going to do, for it to be effective, we must break free from the stronghold of the past. Breaking through will not be easy, because sometimes the problem was passed on to us from our parents or grandparents.

Travelling Through Rough Waters

There is a story about little Bradley. Bradley started first grade, and he was so excited about it. He was outgoing and energetic. He met many new friends, but after a couple of months, Bradley began having intense panic attacks at school. He would get so upset and afraid that his parents had to come back and pick him up from school after dropping him off. Bradley's teacher tried to calm him down by getting Stephen and Susan on the phone to talk to him. But nothing his parents said could calm him down. Time after time his parents would have to rush back to school to pick him up after dropping him off. There was no reason for Bradley's unexplained fear. Stephen and Susan were loving parents and they had never before left him anywhere; nevertheless, the panic attack continued month after month.

The situation got so bad that when Bradley was at home he would not leave his mother's side. He would follow her from room to room. If she was outside, he was right there; if for some reason he could not find her, he would burst into another panic attack. Stephen and Susan were frustrated and heartbroken, wondering what they had done to cause this awful condition and what they could do to help Bradley. One day Stephen was talking with his father, and he was explaining to him the situation about Bradley. It was like a light turned on in the grandfather's mind. "Stephen, I know exactly what is wrong with Bradley. When I was a little boy in first grade, my father died suddenly, and I was so afraid that my mother would have to walk me to school. I would cry so hard, thinking that she may never come back. Many times she would just turn around and take me back home. I believe somehow that Bradley's fears are connected to mine."

Stephen and Susan now realized that Bradley's fear did not originate with him, it had been passed down to him because of the traumatic event in the grandfather's life. Stephen and Susan began to understand that things could get passed down from one generation to the next, even psychological scars (Jer. 31:29). "The father sucks the sour grapes, and the children and grandchildren's teeth shall be set on edge." Please be reminded that I am not saying here that children and grandchildren are paying for their parents' sin, but we all must agree that children and grandchildren do bear some of the parents' psychological scars.

How many of you out there today find a little of your mother in you? How many of you out there find a little of your father or grandfather in you? It may be a good habit and it may be a bad habit. Breaking through the stronghold of the past may take more than just simply trying to push things out of our mind. Some of us may need to get down on our knees and cry out to God. Stephen and Susan had to get down into some serious praying for Bradley, and thank God today God heard their prayer and He came and took Bradley's fear away.

How many of us today are living under a spirit of depression, a spirit of fear, a spirit of discouragement, a spirit of angry temper, and have no real reason to be fearful, no real reason to be depressed, no real reason to be discouraged, and no real reason to be so angry. God is going to do a new thing for us but we must break free from the stronghold of our past. The children of Israel

Travelling Through Rough Waters

no doubt were living with psychological scars from their parents, not to mention their own scars. There were no psychological counselors in those days as they are today. God was their doctor and counselor. If they had a panic attack, they would have to pray; if they had an angry attack, they would have to pray; if they had Alzheimer's and Parkinson's, they would have to pray. For you and I to break through the stronghold of our pasts, so that God's new thing can take effect, we must seek the Lord in prayer.

I know it is not easy for some of us to break through our spirit of revenge and our spirit of anger. Listen to the story of two men who refused to break through the spirit of revenge. Medo-Persia was the second world power and King Ahasuerus honored a man named Haman, a descendant of Agag the Amalekite king, whom Saul, a Jewish king, had captured and killed. The king made Haman prime minister in charge of all the other nobles in the empire.

At Haman's inauguration as prime minister, the king ordered all officials under him to bow whenever he passed through the city gate. They all carried out the king's order except Mordecai who was a Jew.

They asked him, "Why don't you obey the king and bow before Haman? Day after day they kept after Mordecai to do as the king said, but he always refused. Finally he told them that, as a Jew, he couldn't bow before an Amalekite whose ancestors had slaughtered his people. When Haman heard that Mordecai was not bowing before him like the rest of his officials, he became furious. And when he learned that Mordecai was a Jew, he decided to have not only him but all the Jews throughout the empire executed. As the story goes, Haman was the one who eventually got killed because Mordecai outsmarted him. But my point is to show what our psychologically past can do to us, and the damage it can do to others if we do not get rid of the past that haunts us.

Isaiah 41:10 tells us "Fear not, for I am with you, be not dismayed, for I am thy God. I will strengthen thee, I will help thee, I will uphold thee with my right hand of righteousness." Someone said, "Pastor, I don't know how to stop being afraid." The pastor responded, "Go home and get on your knees and tell God that you don't know how to stop being afraid and you need His help." I would like to suggest to you two ways to break the stronghold of the past. Number one, we need to identify the problem and deal with it; and number two, we need to gain strength from the power of our bloodline.

Identifying the Problem and Dealing with It

Saul had a problem, his problem was jealousy. The moment he saw David he was jealous of him. He did not deal with his problem and his problem dealt with him. If you've got a problem, don't try to sweep it under the rug and hope that it will go away. It will not go away. If you are lazy and undisciplined, don't make excuses; just admit it, and say I am going to deal with this problem, by getting up and doing what needs to be done whether you feel like it or not. If you have an anger problem, or if you don't treat other people with respect, don't try to convince yourself that everything is okay; or if other people have the problem, tell yourself that you have a

Travelling Through Rough Waters

problem with disrespecting people and you are going to make some effort to change the way you treat people.

The Bible says, "Confess your faults one with another." This means that you should find a good, mature friend and say to him or her I need your help. I am struggling with an area in my life, and I want you to help me pray about it. Too often we do just the opposite: I am not going to tell anybody about this problem. What would they think about me? I would be embarrassed. Let us swallow our pride, confess our weakness, and get the help we need. We are talking about breaking through the stronghold of the past to prepare for the new thing God has for us.

Robert grew up in a violent and angry home. As a young man he got hooked on drugs and began selling them to support his habit. He lived dangerously and a self-destructive life followed his family's pattern of violence and anger. Then in his mid-twenties, Robert gave his life to the Lord. As he studied the Bible, he began sharing the good news with others and eventually became a pastor, and his church grew rapidly. He became one of the most respected citizens in the community. He traveled and shared the good news of how God changed his life. People did not know that Robert still had a serious anger problem. God had delivered him from all of his bad habits and addiction, but Robert still struggled with uncontrollable anger and rage. He would never show it in the public, but if something went wrong at home he would flew into uncontrollable rage.

Many times something so insignificant would set him

off. He was abusive to his wife. Many times he would throw her up against the wall and abuse her physically and verbally, then when it was all over he came back and begged her to forgive him. Then she would say to him, "Honey, you need help." But he told her, " I am a pastor, I cannot let anybody know about this." Robert needed help because the Devil was ganging up on him. He needed somebody to help him pray. More prayer, more power. I am not saying that you should go and announce it to the world, but you need to find somebody to talk to and pray with you. Don't go to people who like to gossip; go to people who like to pray. Don't go to people who like to get into other people's business; go to people who like to take other people's business to the Lord in prayer.

Robert finally went to a friend who helped him to pray for his problem. As he confessed his faults and stood against the forces of evil, God heard his prayer and set him free, and today Robert is the gentlest man you would ever meet. Robert is now ready for this new thing God is about to do in his life. To break the stronghold of your past, you must first identify your problem and deal with it. It does not matter how long you have been fighting with it, it does not matter how many times you tried and failed; today is a new day.

The Power of Our Bloodline

To break the stronghold of your past, we should take advantage of the strength in our bloodline. Every year they have the Kentucky Derby. The Kentucky Derby is a prestigious horse race for the strongest and the fastest

Travelling Through Rough Waters

horses in the world. I never realized how much time, effort, and resources went into the making of one of those championship horses. I had always thought that the owner or the jockey recognized that a certain horse was fast and gifted, so they decided to enter the Kentucky Derby. But I learned that the development of a champion racehorse takes much more than that. Kentucky Derby horses are not ordinary horses; they are thoroughbreds. They have generation after generation of winner's blood on the inside.

These horses have been carefully studied and bred for generations. The breeders, trainers, and veterinarians search and study data and statistics for fifty to sixty years to check the animal's bloodline. Within the organization, there is a department called "the blood stock agent." His job is to study the bloodline of the animal. This department will focus its attention on the lineage, it will focus on how the father did on a particular race twenty years ago, it will focus on his size and how fast he runs. As much as a million dollars can be spent on one of these horses. The breeders understand that winners don't randomly happen. Winning must be in the blood. From an observer's point a view, the owner wasted all that money, because the horse looks just like an ordinary horse.

But the owner knows that in the blood of that horse there is a proven legacy of over sixty years of championship genes. It's all in the blood. The owner does not concern himself with the horse's initial weakness. He doesn't concern himself with the color of the horse. He doesn't concern himself with the size of the horse. He

Breaking free from the stronghold of my past

doesn't concern himself with the fact that the horse is presently sick. What he is concerned about is the fact that deep down on the inside the horse has the blood of a winner.

That is how God looks at us. God said that He is going to do a new thing in us, not because of any virtue on our part, but because He knows that we have winner's blood running through our spiritual bloodline. He knows that we have flaws. He knows that we have weaknesses. He knows that we are presently sick, but in spite of those undeniable facts He still decides to do a new thing in us. All because He sees winner's blood running through our spiritual lineage. It really does not matter what color our skin is. It really does not matter what our ethnic background is. It really does not matter how many weakness and flaws we may have. Jesus is going to do a new thing because we have the DNA of the Almighty God running through our spiritual bloodline. You and I have come from a long line of champions.

Our Father, who spoke the galaxies into existence, connects Himself to the human family by way of a step-down transformer and we have His DNA running through our spiritual bloodline. Jesus the Son of God, a warrior, and a champion united Himself with the human family and we have His DNA running through our spiritual bloodline. Moses, a champion of faith, stands at the head of the human family and we have his bloodline running through our spiritual heritage. David, a champion of courage—we have his bloodline running through our spiritual heritage. Samson, a champion of supernatural strength—we have his bloodline running through our spiritual heritage.

Travelling Through Rough Waters

Daniel, a man who demonstrated trust in God and captured divine protection—we have his bloodline running through our spiritual heritage. Nehemiah, a champion of determination and persistence—we have his bloodline running through our spiritual heritage.

For the ladies, you have Ester, a champion of sacrificial giving; she was willing to give her life for the cause of God, and you have her bloodline running through your spiritual heritage. You have Rahab, who was willing to put her life on the line to save the spies and enhance the cause of God, and you have her bloodline running through your spiritual heritage. For the New Testament believers, we have Peter, a champion of boldness, and we have his bloodline running through our spiritual heritage. You and I have come from a long line of champions. So God doesn't mind taking chances with us.

God decided to invest in us, because He is looking at our bloodline. He sees the flaws, He sees weaknesses, He knows that we are presently sick, but He is investing in us because He is looking at our bloodline. As we try to break through the stronghold of the past, we need to take courage, because we have winner's blood in our bloodline. We are the descendants of spiritual giants, and we have champion's blood in us, so brace yourself and accept the new challenge that God has for you.

Chapter 19

The Unwanted List

History tells us that the nation of Israel experienced its golden years under the reign of King David. The spirit of prophecy tells us that David's greatest success came from his ability to get the best out of people and ignore the bad. Dealing with people is one of the greatest challenges in the world today. The church suffers a great deal because most of its members do not know how to deal with the different personalities of others. If the church is to be successful, we must learn to understand one another. I believe James had his share with the

Travelling Through Rough Waters

complexities of the human personality when he wrote, "Let your yes be yes and your no be no" (James 5:12). Sometimes we get distracted by the way people are, and sometimes we take it out on the church by leaving the church or neglecting our duties.

In this chapter, I would like to look at nine different types of personalities in the church and society that we all have to deal with in our everyday activities. They are Brother or Mr. Tank; Sister or Ms. Sniper; Brother or Mr. Grenade; Sister or Ms. Maybe; Brother or Mr. Nothing; Brother or Mr. No; Sister or Ms. Complainer; Brother or Mr. Know-It-All; and Sister or Ms. Yes. It is my desire that when we learn about these types of personalities we will not be so shocked when we run into them. Like David, if we are going to be successful as a Christian community in this world and prepare to go to heaven when Jesus comes, we must to learn to deal with these personalities.

Brother or Mr. Tank

Let us start with Brother Tank or Mr. Tank. Brother Tank is the confrontational, angry, and aggressive personality type in your community. These people respond the same way for everything. In their mind, you should not play with people; you must hit them where it hurts. You should let people know who is the boss. These people do not believe in compromise; it's either their way or no way. Haman was a Mr. Tank. We spoke about him in our previous chapter. He was the Prime Minister of the Medo-Persian Empire. He was a descendant of Agag, the Amalekite king, whom Saul, a Jewish King, had captured and killed. The king made Haman prime minister in

The Unwanted List

charge of all the other nobles in the empire. At Haman's inauguration as prime minister, the king ordered all officials under him to bow whenever he passed through the city gate. They all carried out the king's order except Mordecai who was a Jew. When Haman heard that Mordecai was not bowing before him like the rest of his officials, he became furious. He was asked to give some kind of consideration to Mordecai, realizing that he was a Jew and Jews are not allowed to bow to anyone but God, but they pled to no avail. When he learned that Mordecai was a Jew, he decided to have not only him but all the Jews throughout the empire executed, and if it was not for the grace of God, Mr. Haman Tank would have killed every Jew in the Medo Persian Empire. Mr. Tank will have it no other way, but his way.

It was a beautiful day. The sky was clear, and Jim could hear the birds singing outside his window. He was moving forward on a project, and the office was humming with activity and teamwork. Suddenly he heard Mr. Tank coming down the hallway. The ground began to shake at the sound of the tank coming down the hallway. The walls shook. Mr. Tank came in and pointed his finger at Jim and said, "You are an idiot, and a moron. You are incompetent. You are an embarrassment to the human race. You have been working on this project now for over four weeks and you are already three weeks behind. I don't want to hear anymore of your excuses. Pay attention, because this is what you are going to do..." Jim was left sitting among the rubble of his best efforts and good intentions. When Brother Tank comes at you, the first thing you got to do is to hold your ground, stay put,

Travelling Through Rough Waters

don't let him mess up your mind. Aim at the bottom line and fire in the name of Jesus.

Tell Brother Tank in a nice way that he should be ashamed of his behavior. Remind Brother Tank of who he is. From the church's point of view Brother Tank needs to be born again. Angry and bossy people don't go to heaven, but born-again people do. There are a lot of Brother Tanks and Sister Tanks in the church; keep your eyes open for them and sidestep them when they come at you, because when two tanks meet there is an explosion. Members with the tank personalities don't do too well as head of the hospitality committee. They don't do too well as head of any department in the church, because we must be like Jesus to get along with one another.

Sister Sniper

Sister Sniper specializes in rude comments, biting sarcasm, rolling of the eyes, hissing of the teeth, and making you look foolish. Sister Sniper may have a degree and think that everybody else who does not have a college degree is not on her level. Foolish talking and incompetent people she cannot stand. When I was in college, I had a roommate who was a sniper. He would rip people to shreds with his tongue. When he got done with his victim he would disappear and never come back. I saw him rip up one of his victims before. The victim's blood was all over the floor and he looked at me as if to say, I told you, do you see what I can do with my tongue? He never really got the chance to lay hands on me because I am pretty good in side-stepping a sniper.

Sue had never worked this hard in her life to prepare

a report. This was her big day, and if she could deliver her presentation in a professional and polished manner, there was a good chance she could get a promotion. So the day came and she was going through her presentation, everything was fine, all the numbers were in place and victory was in sight. But, just two rows from the front seat she heard a movement like the turning of pages and that was when she heard the first shot, from the sniper: "Hey, that idea reminds me of something I saw in a book. I think it was in chapter eleven or chapter thirteen." Sister Sniper sat there getting ready to take another shot. "Maybe it was from chapter thirteen." Then with a diabolical laugh she said, "Please go on, I am just beginning to understand how little you know about this subject."

Susan's mind wandered. Her concentration was broken and the point she was about to make was lost, and it was a disaster from there on. The sniper hides behind such devious techniques as rude comments, sarcastic humor, piercing looks, unloving tones of voice, rolling of the eyes, and hissing of the teeth. The sniper can use confusion as a weapon by making irrelevant remarks that throw people off track and leave them looking foolish. A few well-placed shots at the right time will put their victim down and the only one left standing will be the sniper.

Sometimes the sniper sits on your Bible-class committee, sometimes the sniper sits on the deacon board, sometimes the sniper sits on the elders' board, sometimes the sniper is a member of the choir, sometimes the sniper is the pastor or his wife, and sometimes the sniper is just a regular member in the church. From the

Travelling Through Rough Waters

church's point of view, Sister Sniper or Brother Sniper needs to be born again, because intelligent people don't go to heaven, but born-again people do go to heaven. God is looking for loving and tender-hearted people in the church. I said, Sister Sniper, you must be born again. Because there should be no snipers in the church.

Some people are not born snipers; they make themselves into snipers. For example, Miriam, the sister of Moses, was not a born sniper, but she was employed by the Devil for a while to do the job of a sniper. God quickly moved in and told her to make up her mind as to whom she is going to work for. This is what happened. She got mad with Moses because he married this beautiful black woman named Zipporah (Exod. 2:21, Num. 12:1). She was the daughter of the priest of Median, Jethro.

Moses lead the people according to God's direction, then Moses heard a little rumbling in the corner and then the shot came, "Hath the Lord indeed spoken only by Moses? Hath he not spoken also by us" (Num. 12:2). She spoke like this because she was upset with Moses. She thought, as a Jew, Moses should have never married this black woman, not to mention these were the same people who had enslaved them in Egypt. God was watching, and before the sniper took another shot He moved in and Miriam became a leper, to show God's disapproval of her job as a sniper. A sniper's shots are devastating. If God did not move in immediately, the whole plan of Moses leading the children of Israel to the promised land could have exploded at the very inception of the plan.

The Unwanted List

Brother Grenade
A grenade is a dangerous thing. It is a little bomb thrown by hand or launched mechanically. The main purpose of the grenade is to instill fear in a fight. People who have the grenade personality just explode into an unfocused rage that has nothing to do with the present situation. Let me give you an example. Mr. Ralph was at his desk working when Mr. Bob walked into the room. His face was rigid, his hand was balled up into a fist. Ralph sensed that something was wrong, but he did not want to say anything. Bob passed by Ralph's desk and the breeze from his body knocked over some books on the desk. Ralph did not mean to say anything, but a little voice escaped his throat: "Careful there, Bob." Bob, still walking around with his facial muscles twitching, his hair standing up on his arms, exploded. "Why don't you watch where you put your stuff? How was I supposed to know that the books were there! That's the problem with the world today. Nobody cares about anything!"

After a while Bob's anger subsided. He stopped yelling, the hair on his arms started going down, and he looked around at everyone staring at him. The books were still on the ground and then he stormed out the door without another word. Brother Bob needs to be born again, because he is out of control. Born-again people are in control of themselves. There are a lot of Bobs in the church today. Sometimes you see people and they get mad at you for no reason. It may be the first time you are seeing these people; however, they are mad at you. I have seen people in my Bible study trying to explain a

Travelling Through Rough Waters

point and another person is trying to help them explain their point and, for no reason, they go off on the person who is trying to help them. You must be aware of the Bob personality, or the grenade personality in the church, on the job, in school, and in society as a whole. If you run into a Bob, or grenade personality don't leave the church or your job because of Bob. Bob needs to be born again, that all.

Brother Know-It-All

Brother Know-It-All has a low tolerance for correction; however, if something goes wrong, Brother Know-It-All will spare no time to speak with authority about who is to be blame. Brother Know-It-All does not think before he speaks, because he knows everything. Brother Samuel ordered an adult large-print lesson quarterly. Brother Samuel was not in church when the quarterly came, so the superintendent sent it to Brother Samuel's home. When Brother Samuel saw the quarterly he realized the superintendent had sent a small-print quarterly to him, so he called the church office to speak to him. George, Brother Know-It-All, picked up the phone. Brother Samuel began to explain to him that it seemed as if the superintendent had made a mistake by sending him the wrong quarterly. George, the Mr. Know-It-All, began to explain to Brother Samuel that it seemed as if he had made the mistake of ordering the wrong quarterly. The conversation got so heated between both men that Brother Samuel stopped coming to church and it took the pastor many months to get Brother Samuel to start coming back to church.

The Unwanted List

Here is another one. Dave bought a piece of software from a computer company, where Brother Frank, the Know-It-All, was working. Dave called the company to inform them that the software was not working. Frank took the call, and after Dave explained to him the problem he was having with the software, Frank, the Know-It-All, said to him, "It seems to me that you are having a mechanical problem, not a software problem." Dave said, "No, it's not my computer because other software runs very well on it." Mr. Know-It-All said to him, "Listen to me, I've worked on hundreds of software and what you described to me is a software problem. Can you tell me which extension you loaded onto your computer?" Dave said, "Sir, I am telling you it is not a software problem." Frank, the Know-It-All responded, "Sir, that is what I am trying to determine." Dave said, "How do you know it is not a software problem?" Mr. Know-It-All responded, "Sir, you are not listening to me. It is not a software problem. The problem is with your computer." Dave finally had to ask to speak to the supervisor. You will get nowhere with Mr. Know-It-All. I am trying to show you the type of people who you have to deal with in the church, on the job, and in your home. I am trying to share with you these different traits and personalities so that you won't get so frustrated with people.

If I tell you about Brother Tank, Sister Sniper, and Brother Know-It-All, when you run into them in the church or in society, don't be mad with them; just say, Oh, I heard about you, and move on. Some people get so mad when they run into Brother Tank or Sister Sniper, then they say, I am not coming back to church, they are

Travelling Through Rough Waters

all nothing more than a bunch of hypocrites. Why are you going to let Sister Sniper drive you away from your Father's house? Sister Sniper just needs to be born again, that's all! You see, if you know the way people are, you don't need to get so frustrated and lose your soul.

Oftentimes Mr. or Ms. Know-It-All are knowledgeable and extremely competent people. They are outspoken, and they intend to get the job done in the way they have predetermined. They are very controlling, with a low tolerance for correction. When their decisions and opinions are challenged by new ideas, it is perceived as a threat. Mr. Know-It-All believes that to be wrong is very humiliating. Mr. Know-It-All may have to be born again, because he is making everybody around him miserable.

Brother or Mr. Nothing

Brother or Sister Nothing are people who have nothing to say; they just sit there and look. These people are not necessarily ignorant. Some of these people are educated people; however, most of the time they have nothing to say. They sit and look at you, occasionally smile, and have nothing much to say. I know that the Bible says, "He that keeps his lips, keeps his life" (Prov. 13:3). Even then, Mr. Nothing must understand that the Bible is right, but God did not mean that a person says nothing. It is wise not to talk too much, but the same people who agree with this will think you are foolish if you do not say anything when you should have said something. You may find these people on your job, in your school, in the church, and in your family or at home.

Here is a scenario with Mr. Nothing. The first elder

The Unwanted List

of the Bethel Seventh-day Adventist Church in a certain city is practicing witchcraft. Now, if you know anything about Seventh-day Adventist people, you will know that is a no-no. A good Adventist does not practice black magic. Back in Bible days, Sabbath-keepers used to stone their members who were caught practicing witchcraft. Even God gets upset when His people go to see a witch or practice witchcraft. He punished a whole nation of people for practicing witchcraft.

Let me show you what He said. In Jeremiah 14: We see Jeremiah reasoning with the Lord. He told God that He stood motionless like a surprised man, like a warrior who cannot save others. The people are in trouble and God does nothing to help them, so Jeremiah is reasoning with God as to why He does not help the people. This is what the Lord told Jeremiah, "These people love to go to their foreign gods. They cannot control their own feet. I am not pleased with what they have done to themselves and against me. I will not overlook their sin, but I will let them reap what they have sown. So don't pray for these people, asking me to help them; they are beyond help. Even if they fast and pray, I will not listen to them. Even if they bring offerings and sacrifice, I will not accept their worship; instead, I will allow them to be consumed by war, famine and disease" (Jer. 14:10-12). So, you can see that God is very upset when His people consult witches. God calls the action a sin.

Let's go back to Brother Nothing. Some of the leaders of the church decided to call a meeting to discuss a process of how to approach the first elder. Brother Nothing was asked to be at the meeting, because he was

Travelling Through Rough Waters

a key witness. Brother Nothing lived not far from the witch and he had seen the elder many times going to the witch's house late at night. The chairperson called the meeting to order and introduced the subject matter. He asked if anyone had any suggestion of how to approach the first elder about his behavior. One of the members asked a question. He said, "Do we have any concrete evidence that the elder has been practicing witchcraft? This is a serious issue and we want to be right when we approach him." The chairperson said, "Yes, we do, Brother Nothing has seen the elder several times going to the witch's house late at night." Another member responded, "Is that true, Brother Nothing?" Brother Nothing just sat there looking; he smiled a few times and just looked at the beautiful chandelier lights hanging from the ceiling of the church.

Someone suggested that they bring the meeting to a close because there was not enough evidence to approach the first elder of the church. When you run into Mr. Nothing or Ms. Nothing, do not allow your blood pressure to go up; just keep in mind that there are people in this world like Mr. Nothing. I said previously that the Nothings are not necessarily ignorant; they may be educated people. Their nature is to say nothing, so the most you will get out of these people is nothing. Try not to put Mr. Nothing on the conflict-resolution team. Try not to put Ms. Nothing as head of the ICC unit. Try not to use Pastor Nothing to speak at the youth convention, because these people will say nothing.

Brother or Mr. No

The Unwanted List

Many years ago when my first daughter was much younger, my niece was living at home with us, so they both joined together in finding ways of how to get money from me after they had spent their allowance. Each time they came to me and asked for money I would tell them, "I do not have any money." One day my daughter said to me, "Daddy, are these the only words you know?" So I said to her, "What words?" She said to me, "I don't have any money." Then I realized that I was using my line of defense too often. She came to realize that this was my way of not giving up any more money, so I would tell them that I did not have money without even thinking about it. Mr. No and Ms. No are people who say no without even thinking about why they are saying no.

Come with me and let us look at Mr. No in action. The youth pastor of the First Baptist Missionary Church in a certain city wanted to take the youth of the church to Disney World, but he was having problems with transportation. The church had a bus, but it was just a fifteen-seater, so there would not be enough space for everybody. The youth pastor called a meeting to discuss the situation. Someone suggested to drive the church bus and asked some of the parents who would like to drive their SUVs and help out with the youth. Another person said that she was speaking with a person from the charter-bus company in town and from what the person told her, it seemed as if it would be much more economical to take the charter bus. Not to mention, the youth would like to be with their friends on the trip. Many of the members asked questions about the driving history of the bus company and pricing.

Travelling Through Rough Waters

They all seemed to be satisfied with the idea and the pastor was about to call for a vote, when from corner of the room everyone could hear the voice of Mr. No: "It will not work." The pastor asked Brother No what was the reason for his objection. He said to the pastor, "I just know Sister Roger's idea will not work." The pastor went on with the vote, the idea passed, and the youth were able to go to Disney World—but Brother No did not go with them. Some of the time, the No people do not have a reason to say no, it is their nature to say no. This is not to say that the No people do not have a valid point for saying no sometimes. My point is, not to get upset when people say no when you think that they should say yes or the circumstances warrant them to say yes.

Sister or Ms. Complainer

Sister Complainer or Brother Complainer are the types of people who are chronic complainers. If things do not go the way they want it to go, they never stop complaining. Complainers can cause problems by complaining to everyone. Complainers seem to be not as dangerous as snipers or some other personality traits, but sometimes they can be even more dangerous. After Lucifer became discontented in heaven, he went around complaining to the other angels in heaven about God's unfairness with him, and this behavior, as simple as it looked then, caused a third of all the angels in heaven to be thrown out of heaven (Rev. 12:4). This is what Ellen G. White tells us in *Story of Redemption:*

Lucifer in heaven, before his rebellion, was a high and exalted angel, next in honor to God's dear Son. His countenance, like those of the other angels, was mild and expressive of happiness. His forehead was high and broad, showing a powerful intellect. His form was perfect; his bearing noble and majestic. A special light beamed in his countenance and shone around him brighter and more beautiful than around the other angels; yet Christ, God's dear Son, had the pre-eminence over all the angelic host. He was one with the Father before the angels were created. Lucifer was envious of Christ, and gradually assumed command which devolved on Christ alone.

Lucifer was envious and jealous of Jesus Christ. Yet when all the angels bowed to Jesus to acknowledge His supremacy and high authority and rightful rule, he bowed with them; but his heart was filled with envy and hatred. Christ had been taken into the special counsel of God in regard to His plans, while Lucifer was unacquainted with them. He did not understand, neither was he permitted to know, the purposes of God. But Christ was acknowledged sovereign of heaven, His power and authority to be the same as that of God Himself.

Lucifer thought that he was himself a favorite in heaven among the angels. He had been highly exalted, but this did not call forth from him gratitude and praise to his Creator. He aspired to the height of God Himself. He gloried in his loftiness. He knew that he was honored by the angels. He had a special mission to execute. He had been near the great Creator, and the ceaseless beams of glorious light enshrouding the eternal God had shone especially upon him. He thought how angels had obeyed his command with pleasurable alacrity. Were not his garments light and beautiful? Why should Christ thus be

Travelling Through Rough Waters

honored before himself?

He left the immediate presence of the Father, dissatisfied and filled with envy against Jesus Christ. Concealing his real purposes, he assembled the angelic host. He introduced his subject, which was himself. (He is complaining to the angels.) As one aggrieved, he related the preference God had given Jesus to the neglect of himself. He told them that henceforth all the sweet liberty the angels had enjoyed was at an end. For had not a ruler been appointed over them, to whom they from henceforth must yield servile honor? He stated to them that he had called them together to assure them that he no longer would submit to this invasion of his rights and theirs; that never would he again bow down to Christ; that he would take the honor upon himself which should have been conferred upon him, and would be the commander of all who would submit to follow him and obey his voice.

There was contention among the angels. Lucifer and his sympathizers were striving to reform the government of God. They were discontented and unhappy because they could not look into His unsearchable wisdom and ascertain His purposes in exalting His Son, and endowing Him with such unlimited power and command. They rebelled against the authority of the Son. Angels that were loyal and true sought to reconcile this mighty, rebellious angel to the will of his Creator. They justified the act of God in conferring honor upon Christ, and with forcible reasoning sought to convince Lucifer that no less honor was his now than before the Father had proclaimed the honor which He had conferred upon His

The Unwanted List

Son.

They clearly set forth that Christ was the Son of God, existing with Him before the angels were created; and that He had ever stood at the right hand of God, and His mild, loving authority had not heretofore been questioned; and that He had given no commands but what it was joy for the heavenly host to execute. They urged that Christ's receiving special honor from the Father, in the presence of the angels, did not detract from the honor that Lucifer had heretofore received. The angels wept. They anxiously sought to move him to renounce his wicked design and yield submission to their Creator; for all had heretofore been peace and harmony, and what could occasion this dissenting, rebellious voice? Lucifer refused to listen. And then he turned from the loyal and true angels, denouncing them as slaves. These angels, true to God, stood in amazement as they saw that Lucifer was successful in his effort to incite rebellion.

Complainers can disrupt the overall plan of the church or the group. Sister Bomaram had a long family heritage in the Shiloh Baptist Church in a certain city. As a matter of fact, her father had built the first church where the people are now worshiping. Sister Bomaram knew pretty much everyone in the church. She spoke to the church conference secretary every week, not to mention the pastor who she called daily. The church has outgrown its present capacity and the members voted to build a new church. A building committee was formed and Sister Bomaram was elected as one of the members. In their discussion, the building committee talked about moving the new church to another spot on the same

Travelling Through Rough Waters

property. Sister Bomaram rejected the idea and fought hard to persuade the building committee not to change the spot of the new church. She was outvoted and the committee agreed to move the new church to another spot on the same property.

Sister Bomaram started calling everybody in the church and complained to them, how the building committee did a terrible thing in changing the spot where her father had chosen seventy-five years ago to put the new church. She called the pastor so many times that he had to highlight her name on his phone, so that he could know when she was calling. Her friend at the conference office had to do the same thing too. Sister Bomaram would take folks home after church for dinner and while they were eating, the conversation would be on the building committee's decision to change the spot for the new church. Sister Bomaram finally left the church and a few other people with her and started attending another church. Thank God she continued to go to a church, but as you can see, complainers can disrupt the plan and in some cases, cause destruction of the church or whatever the complainer may be dissatisfied about. When you run into Ms. or Mr. Complainer, be gentle with them, but do not let them deter you. Most complainers are selfish. Most times the complainer can only see what he or she wants. The complainer must understand that even though his idea may be a great idea he should also be a good team player for the benefit of the project.

Sister or Ms. Yes
Ms. Yes and Mr. Yes are people you will meet who will tell

The Unwanted List

you yes without thinking about whether they can actually do what they tell you they are going to do. Mr. Yes and Ms. Yes create problems for other people by agreeing to do things that they know they cannot do. Sister Walker is the director of the human resource office of the Ford Motor Company in a certain town. She is also a member of the First Baptist Church in said town. The First Baptist Church has a membership of 2500. The pastor of the church asked Sister Walker to serve as church secretary. Sister Walker knew that to serve as the church secretary of such a large outfit would be very difficult for her due to her job as director of the human resource department at her job; however, she took the position.

The Ford Motor Company was preparing for their new release on the first of the New Year and they asked their employees to put in some overtime to help the company reach their goal. They were also hiring new employees and the human resource office was very busy. At the same time, the First Baptist Church was having an election of officers for the New Year. The pastor always wanted the head church secretary to be a part of the nominating committee. Reality came home to Sister Walker. By trying to juggle between these two positions, Sister Walker had a nervous breakdown and wound up in the hospital for three weeks. During her stay in the hospital, both the Ford Motor Company and the church suffered because the church did not have a head secretary and the Ford Motor Company did not have a human resource director.

All of this could have been avoided if Sister Yes had just said no when she was not able to do something.

Travelling Through Rough Waters

Mr. Yes and Ms. Yes do not like to hurt people's feelings, so most of the time they say yes without even thinking. Please watch out for the Mr. Yes and the Ms. Yes. Your frustration level will remain low if you are on the lookout for the Mr. Yes and the Ms. Yes who will frustrate your plans by accepting a position that they know they cannot do. Please be reminded that most of the Yeses are good people, so don't hurt their feelings; just be aware that these people are out there and prepare yourself for these situations. The personalities of the human family are vast. I have just scratched the surface and I hope I have helped you even in a small way. By understanding one another, we develop brotherly cohesiveness, then all our plans will run smooth and effectively.

Chapter 20

If My People Would Pray

If my people pray, I will hear from heaven and I will forgive their sin. Our worship service is a dynamic entity, but many of us haven't the slightest idea of what takes place in our worship service and our place in the worship service. In the Book of II Chronicles we find a vivid view of this power that is available to the people of God during the worship service. In 2 Chronicles 7:1-3, we see the people gather for worship and Solomon praying on

Travelling Through Rough Waters

behalf of the people and the country. At the moment of prayer God's presence and glory filled the temple and the people fell on their knees and worshiped Him. God's presence is no less with His people today than in the days of old, but today many of the members of God's church have little or no idea or expectation when they come to worship. Some people come to the worship service because they were told to come. They have no plan and they have no expectation, so they come in dry and they leave dry.

Solomon asked the Lord to make provisions for the people when they go into battle and when they sin, because he was afraid that because of the people's sin they would be defeated in battle and they would be taken captive to other countries and while they were there they might have a change of heart, or they would turn away from God. It was months, maybe years after Solomon's prayer when the Lord came to him one night and told him, "I have heard thy prayer." After all this time. If you notice the text, 2 Chronicles 7:11, Solomon finished the temple and did other things that he had in mind to do. Then the Lord came and told him "I have heard thy prayer." How many times have we given up on God because He did not come through at a time that you have set? How often do we look for immediate answers to our prayers and when nothing happens we wonder if God has heard our prayer?

How many times have you gotten upset with God because you think that your prayer should have been answered long ago? God hears all our requests and He will do so for us. We must trust God and believe that

If My People Would Pray

he will answer at the proper time. The worship service is of vital importance to all of us. We should never miss an appointment with God. God does not put our prayer requests on His desk until He is able to get to it, or lets it wait so He can respond to other things. Our requests are placed in His active file and a time has been appointed for that particular request to be carried out. You and I must have faith in the system. It works, don't let time interfere with your faith in God's ability to deliver us from our troubles. In 2 Chronicles 6, Solomon made his request to God on behalf of the people and the country. In 2 Chronicles 7, the Lord responded to Solomon's request. His decision to respond to the request was based on four conditions, and these same conditions apply to us today. God said, For Me to hear the prayers of the saints:

They should humble themselves,
They should pray and ask for forgiveness,
They should seek God continually, and turn from their wicked ways.

If My people who are called by My name humble themselves and pray and turn from their wicked ways looking to Me for help, I will hear from heaven and I will forgive them of their sins and heal their land. People who are called by My name, a person's name means a lot to them. Nobody wants to have a bad name. A name means a lot. When Abraham's son asked him where he was going to get the lamb for the sacrifice, Abraham told the boy Jehovah-Jireh, meaning, "The Lord will provide."

Travelling Through Rough Waters

God's name has to do with His ability to provide for His people. Eli's daughter-in-law was pregnant and when she heard that her husband had died in the battle, she had a premature delivery and she named her son "Ichabod," which means the glory of God has departed from Israel. The boy's name has to do with his inability to preform. Those whose lives are torn with guilt, broken vows, an abusive past, a ruined relationship—we tell them, "Jehovah Shalom," meaning God is peace, Jesus will save you and give you peace in spite of your past. But what exactly does God mean when He says, "My people who are called by My name?"

It means that God has chosen you and me to represent Him in this world. When we publicly declare our love for Christ through baptism, we join those who are called by His name. You and I should protect God's name. You and I should protect God's reputation. We should not do anything that would discredit the name of Christ. God wants us to protect His name and because we have His name He considers us a part of the heavenly family. I have four children and two grandchildren and if any of my kids does something disgraceful, it brings a dark cloud over the family's reputation, so we protect our family by trying to do the right thing. We are not perfect, but we try to keep the family reputation. God has a family, and He adopted us into His family through the blood of Jesus Christ, and He asked us to protect the family's reputation.

Let us look at the conditions God has laid down for one to get a prayer through. After Solomon prayed, God came to him in a dream and said, "If My people who are

If My People Would Pray

called by My name humble themselves and pray and turn from their wicked ways looking to Me for help, I will hear from heaven and I will forgive them of their sins and heal their land." So condition one:

They Should Humble Themselves

The first thing we got to do so that we can hear from heaven, we must humble ourselves before God. Many of us are strong-headed and we do whatever we feel like doing. A little girl once was sitting at the table waiting for the rest of the family who were going to a choir rehearsal. She was looking at some Bible stories. She looked up at her dad and said, "Dad, are you a government?" Her dad said, "No, why?" She said, "Oh, well, I wish you were a government." "Why is that?" the father replied. "Because then Candi and I could do whatever we want to do. Everybody else would have to obey, but we would not have to because you are the government and you are our father." Some Christians feel and think the same way. They feel that their status as children of God somehow entitles them to be above the law. They are exempt from being obedient.

But I would like to think that our relationship with our Father in heaven is similar to the relationship that was shared by Robert and John F. Kennedy during the Kennedy Administration in the U.S. The two men were brothers and bonded by blood. There was a special understanding between both. Bobby, as the attorney general, was clearly subservient to his brother John. John was his commander in chief and Bobby was subject to John's authority, but Bobby had no problem with that. Because

Travelling Through Rough Waters

of their special bond and relationship as brothers, Bobby was also acknowledged as the president's closest advisor. Both men shared many thoughts and ideas about the running of the country. John's position was to be lord over his brother and Bobby understood this and allowed his brother John to be lord over him. They were fulfilling a role in government, but it was also a relationship that allowed Bobby access to the inner chamber of the world seat of power.

Some people cannot stand for their relative to be lord over them. They feel belittled, but that is the spirit of the Devil. If God has raised up your brother (or your sister) to be a leader over His people and you are a part of these people, then he is also leader over you and you ought to give him the respect that is due to him. God is very displeased when we disrespect each other, particularly those whom He has set as leaders over His people. Come with me and I'll show you how God truly feels about this attitude.

In the Book of Numbers, chapter 12, we find a situation that warranted God's immediate presence. [I told the story earlier, but I must tell it again to make a point] Moses and his brother and sister were the top leaders in leading out in the exodus of the children of Israel, but Miriam had a problem; she was upset with her brother Moses because Moses went and married a beautiful black woman (Num. 12:1-2). Miriam thought that Moses should not have anything to do with this black woman, not to mention these were the same people who had enslaved them in Egypt and her brother had the nerve to marry one of them!

If My People Would Pray

Miriam started it and Aaron followed. God heard their disrespect toward His elected leader and this is what happened: So the Lord called Moses, Miriam, and Aaron to come into the courtyard and stand by the entrance of the sanctuary. The Lord came down and settled over the sanctuary where the three of them stood and He asked Miriam and Aaron to step forward. Then the Lord said to the two of them, "Listen to me. When I choose someone to be a prophet I reveal myself to him in visions and speak to him in dreams. But my servant Moses is different. I have put him in charge of all the people and he has faithfully done what I have told him to do. I don't speak to him in visions and dreams that people can question, but talk with him plainly, as two men face each other to talk together. I have allowed him only to see my back and protected him so he would not die when he saw me. On what basis then, do you have a right to be jealous and feel neglected because there were times he didn't consult you before doing what I asked him to do? Why would you blame his wife for this?" The Lord was very displeased with them, particularly with Miriam who had started all this with her seditious whispering. Then the Lord's cloud lifted. When it did, Miriam was covered with disease that looked like leprosy, and her whole body turned deathly white. When Aaron saw what had happened to his sister, he felt severely rebuked for listening to her and said to Moses, Please forgive us! Don't hold this sin against us! We have been fools and were led astray by jealousy. We admit we were wrong and that we have sinned against the Lord. Don't let Miriam's body look like a baby born dead, whose body is

Travelling Through Rough Waters

partially decomposed when it comes out of the womb. Then Moses pled with the Lord, praying, "O Lord, please forgive her and heal her!" The Lord answered, "If her father had spit in her face to show his displeasure with her wickedness, as the custom is, would she not be ashamed in the eyes of the people and have to live away from the camp for seven days? Let Miriam do the same now. Send her out of the camp for seven days. After that she can come back." This story is a strong rebuke to anyone who take it upon themselves to disrespect God's chosen leaders.

As God's children, we are his servants, we are His friends, we are His brothers, collaborators, priests, and kings. Jesus is Lord, we are His brothers and sisters, but He is Lord. He is still the head. We must understand how the system works. We are still subject to Him. We come under His rulership and His management. At the same time we have unrestricted access into the throne room of the universe. We must humble ourselves before God. Don't step over your bounds and expect God to overlook because we are kin and bonded by blood. Jesus is the President, He is the Commander in Chief, and a good brother will obey his brother who is the president. We are talking about humbling yourself before God.

They Should Pray and Ask for Forgiveness

Secondly, for us to hear from heaven we must pray and ask God to forgive us of our sin. Not only should we humble ourselves, but we ought to pray and ask God to forgive us of our sin. Many people cannot pray. Their prayers are nothing more than a recitation. They have

If My People Would Pray

a prayer book in their minds. That is not prayer. Prayer ought not be from memory. Prayer should be alive, meaning you think and feel as you pray. Pray what you feel, pray what you understand, and pray what you are thinking. If you don't feel anything, and if you don't think anything, and if you don't see anything, you have only one alternative and that is to ask God to teach you how to pray.

Don't be ashamed to tell God exactly where you are. Tell Him you should be praying, but you don't know how to pray, and you are asking Him for a jumpstart. When God said, "If my people would pray." What he means is, if my people would talk to me, if they would take a little time out and talk to me, then they would hear from heaven.

Some people do not have time to talk to God except for when they are in trouble, but that is okay too; if that is the only way He can get you to talk to Him, he will give you trouble. There is something else I would like to say to you. There are a lot of people today who are getting this attitude of being mad with the Lord. Don't do that. God is not your equal, and He will not be trifled with. God is not a man that He should lie. He is God, and when we find ourselves getting mad with Him we are simply saying He is our equal and He is not omniscient. If God knows best, why would you be so upset with Him when He works on your behalf? When the idea comes to your mind to get upset with God, resist it, and pray like David: "Have mercy on me, O God, according to your loving-kindness, according to your abundant mercy, blot out my sin. Wash away my guilt and cleanse me from

Travelling Through Rough Waters

sin. I know my weakness and I am conscious of my sinful nature. Lord, please have mercy upon me."

They Should Seek God Continually
God also said that for us to hear from heaven we need to seek His face or seek God continually. Seeking God's face or seeking God continually is to have an active relationship with Him and this does not mean coming to church every week. Some people feel pride in the fact that they come to church every week, but it does not get them anywhere, because they are the biggest devils in the church. You know that some people are addicted to coming to church. They've got to go to church. It doesn't mean that it is doing anything for them, but they just got to be in church. Well, we are not talking about that kind of relationship this morning. Our religion should do something for us.

If our religion cannot restrain us,

If our religion cannot help us to be a nice person to other people,

If you find the church to be boring and you always depend on someone else to make you feel good in church, your relationship with God is sick and it needs to go to the doctor. God does not like sick relationships.

God does not like for the angels to bring bad news to heaven everyday about what is going on in your house. He does not like the idea that the angels have to step out of your home because of what is going on in there. Listen to this: "Angels are hovering around yonder dwelling. The young are there assembled; there is the sound of vocal and instrumental music. Christians are gathered there, but what is that you hear? It is a song, a frivolous ditty, fit for the dance hall. Behold, the pure angels gather their light closer around them, and darkness envelops those in that dwelling. The angels are moving from the scene. Sadness is upon their countenances. Behold, they are weeping. This I saw repeated a number of times all through the ranks of Christians." (Ellen G. White, *Messages to Young People,* Ch. "A wrong use of music") If your religion does not bring joy to your heart you will not be able to seek God's face and you will not hear from heaven. Someone said, it is not who you know, but who knows you. God needs to know you personally so you can hear from heaven.

Turn From Your Wicked Ways

The final step in the process of hearing from heaven is that you must turn from your wicked ways. God told Solomon, for Him to answer the people's prayers, the people would have to turn from their wicked ways. You cannot expect to hear from heaven if you are wicked and doing wicked things. In other words, if you want to hear from God you need to work hard on doing the right thing. God is not there to condemn us when we slip or make a mistake, but some people live a slipping life, and they do not plan to change. That is their Christianity. In their mind, that should suffice. Somebody said, I cannot change, I tried, but I found myself right back where I was. I am getting to the place where I am accepting my lifestyle. I do not think that I can change. Maybe my probation is closed.

I present to you today the words of a songwriter:

Travelling Through Rough Waters

"Would you be free from your burden of sin, there is power in the blood. Come now for cleansing at Calvary spring, there is wonderful power in the blood. There is power, power, wonder-working power in the blood of the Lamb. There is power, power, wonder-working power in the precious blood of the Lamb." God told Solomon, these are the conditions for one to hear from heaven:
Humble yourself before God.
Pray and ask God to forgive your sin.
Seek God's face = Have a relationship with Me.
Turn from your wicked ways.

Then he/she will hear from heaven. Solomon, I heard your prayer and I know you mean good, but I have some conditions. My people will have to abide by these conditions to hear from heaven. Not only will that man or that woman hear from heaven, but I will be in church with them and they will experience my joy in worship. I will listen when they pray from the church and I will answer their prayer. I will make you prosperous in all that you do. Some people say I am already prospering; well it may seem as if you are prospering, but your prosperity is only temporary. No one has permanent prosperity except that God gives it to them. God is willing today to carry out the promise He had made with the people of Israel and with you and me. Those of us who are called by His name, if we humble ourselves and pray, if we turn our hearts toward home, God will hear us from heaven. And He will respond to all our needs.

Chapter 21

How Does One Get to Be in God's Hall of Fame?

I looked up the phrase, "Hall of Fame," and I notice that it is a place where celebrities are honored. I thought to myself, I do not fit into this categories of people. First of all, I do not have much to offer, and secondly, I am not gifted with the things that the people of the world love.

Travelling Through Rough Waters

So I decided to look and see if God has a Hall of Fame, and if He does how can I get into His Hall of Fame. And that's when Paul directed my attention to the Book of Hebrews. Hebrews 11:1-6 tells us that God does have a Hall of Fame and it is possible for us to be in it. In this chapter I shall look at a few people who were inducted into God's Hall of Fame and the process they went through to be inducted. The Bible mentions Abel, Abraham, Jacob, Sarah, Moses, Rahab, Gideon, and David, just to mention a few. Let us take them one by one and address their qualifications. I shall look carefully at how they were qualified to be in God's Hall of Fame.

Abel's Qualification to God's Hall of Fame

"By faith we understand that God created the whole universe out of nothing. So the things we see were made out of things that didn't exist. This is the kind of faith that Abel had when he sacrificed a lamb and added grain, but Cain offered the grain without the lamb. So Abel won God's approval as being righteous because he showed his faith in God by what he did. God was pleased. (Heb. 11:3-4)

Adam was thrown out of the Garden of Eden (Gen. 3:23-24). Ellen G. White, tells us Adam and Eve took their children to the gate of the garden and worshiped God every day. "Cain and Abel, the sons of Adam, were very unlike in character. Abel feared God. Cain cherished rebellious feelings and murmured against God because of the curse pronounced upon Adam and because the ground was cursed for his sin" (*Story of Redemption*, "Cain and Abel"). Cain was upset with God, and being

How Does One Get to Be in God's Hall of Fame?

the elder brother he no doubt had a lot of influence on his brother Abel, so he sought to draw him into a controversy with God. Cain was mad with God because God put his father and mother out of their beautiful home. And he was trying to show his brother how unfair God was and every time he brought up the conversation Abel was telling him that he should not say that, because God is just and He does the right thing.

I can imagine Cain argued with his brother Abel, what do you know about God, have you ever seen God? Has God ever done anything for you? Look at us, our parents told us what God did to them, and for some unknown reason I cannot get it into your head that God is not fair. Abel might have responded, I may not know a lot about God, I may never have seen God, but there is something within me that we call faith; it is a substance that cannot be felt, but it is the evidence of things hoped for, and this thing within me that is called faith, it tells me that God is just, He is honest and He is pure, so, Cain, I just cannot accept your philosophy about God.

As they worshiped week by week, Cain brought the fruits of the field as an offering to the Lord—symbolic of his own labor and given as a favor to God. He refused to ask his brother for a lamb in order to sacrifice an offering as the Lord had instructed his parents to do. But Abel brought a lamb to the Lord, and God accepted Abel's offering because it pointed forward to the One who would give His life for man. Abel understood the principle of redemption and, by his obedience, showed faith in what God had promised to do. But Cain's offering was not acceptable to God. He saw no need for the sacrifice

Travelling Through Rough Waters

of blood. He believed that offering the fruit of his labor was all that mattered. When Cain realized that God was not pleased with his offering, he not only became upset with God, but blamed his brother as well. As time went on, he became increasingly angry....he asked his brother to meet him in the field. When they met, he turned on Abel and killed him." (Gen. 4:1-8, *Clear Word Bible*)

There is more than one way to be inducted into God's Hall of Fame, but first we must have faith in God and do exactly what He asks us to do. People who are in God's Hall of Fame are disciplined; they obey God's word and they are not afraid to stand up for what is right. "Cain, you and I are brothers, but I do not see things the way you do." Some people cannot accept the fact that another person sees things different from them. Cain was one of these people, so he killed his brother. Abel had faith in God's word. He believed that God is good, God is just, God is pure, and his brother's attitude about God was wrong. This was how Abel felt about God, and his attitude about God qualified him to be inducted into God's Hall of Fame.

Abraham's Qualification to God's Hall of Fame

When Abraham was called to leave the comforts of his home in Ur to live in tents in a land he was supposed to inherit, he obeyed, even though he didn't know exactly the place where he was going. By faith he lived in tents in a land God had promised to give him. He lived there as a foreigner, together with Isaac and Jacob, who were heirs of the same promise. By faith he looked forward with

How Does One Get to Be in God's Hall of Fame?

confidence to a city with lasting foundations whose designer and builder is God. (Heb. 11:8-10, *Clear Word Bible*)

Most of Noah's descendants moved eastward to the city of Ur, which today we understand to be a part of Babylon. While in Babylon, or Ur, Shem maintained his father's faith and taught it to his children. Shem was the grandfather of Abraham, so Abraham was brought up to serve the true and living God. Abraham was now seventy-five years old and God told him to get everything that belonged to him and leave his home for the land of Canaan. Abraham obeyed God and went to Canaan. On his way to Canaan his father died. God told Abraham that He would make him the father of a great nation; however, Abraham was now seventy-five and he and his wife had no children. Not long after Abraham got to Canaan, there was a famine in the land, so he traveled to Egypt. When he got to Egypt he had to lie to stay alive, at least he thought that he had to lie to stay alive.

After some time in Egypt Abraham left and went back to Canaan. As soon as Abraham got back to Canaan, there were some tribal wars among the kings, and Lot, his nephew, was taken as a slave. Abraham gathered his men and went after them and rescued his nephew. Melchizedek met him on his way and gave him God's approval for rescuing his nephew. Many years passed since God promised Abraham and God did nothing for Abraham. Abraham reminded God of His promise and God told him, Don't worry about it, you will be a father of many nations. I wonder if you are tracing the steps of Abraham, steps that seem so familiar to many of us. The way God leads us many times seems so unfear, but we

Travelling Through Rough Waters

must let God do the leading and we follow. Sarah was now about eighty years old and she had pretty much given up on God. Out of desperation she negotiated with her husband to sign a surrogate mother contract. Abraham concluded that his wife's idea would resolve the problem.

Thirteen years later the Lord came to Abraham and told him, I will carry out my plan with you if you stop trying to help me do my business (Gen. 17:1-2). Abraham was now ninety-nine years old. Sarah was now about ninety-five and she became pregnant and gave birth to a son. Abraham named him Isaac, which means, "He made me laugh." Abraham raised the boy with such pride and dignity. Everything he owned belonged to this boy. Sarah walked with pride in her steps among the women of her town. Isaac was only about sixteen or eighteen years old when one night the Lord came back to Abraham and told him to take Isaac to Mount Moriah and offer him as a human sacrifice. It took Abraham two days to get to Mount Moriah, and during those two days as he traveled to the mountain he was thinking in his mind, How can God ask me to take the life of my only son. Should I obey God's word and suffer this loss?

We are talking about been chosen to be in God's Hall of Fame. Are you able to walk in Abraham's shoes? Would you travel those lonely roads for those two days to take the life of your only child? Have you ever been called by God, and you found yourself having more trouble than you had before? Does it seem as if God does not care about you and your problems sometimes? You remember Abraham; the things that meant so much to

How Does One Get to Be in God's Hall of Fame?

him, God asked him to give it up. Does He really care? Yes, he does, but that is the road that leads to God's Hall of Fame for some people. Abraham was inducted into God's Hall of Fame because he went where God sent him and he did not complain about it. What about you—do you think that you could get your pass into God's Hall of Fame by doing what God tells you to do without complaining about it?

Jacob's Qualification to God's Hall of Fame

By faith Jacob included the two sons of Joseph in his fatherly blessing as he was dying. He then leaned on his staff as he bowed and worshiped. Joseph also gave evidence of this same faith when, just before he died, he told the Israelites that one day they would leave Egypt and when they leave, they should take his body with them. (Heb. 11:21-22)

Jacob was one of the last persons anyone thought about being in God's Hall of fame. As a matter of fact, he was born with a lying nature, and a thieving mentality. He plotted with his mother to steal his brother's birthrights, and he tricked his father and got the blessing that belonged to his brother. He outsmarted Laban and got the strongest animals. But there is something about him that we cannot deny. In spite of his weakness he held on to the Lord. Just before meeting his brother after thirty years in hiding, he sent his wives and children across the Jab-bok River. He stayed alone that night to talk with Jesus. Jacob lay on his back looking up at the starry heaven. There came a man whom he might have thought was his brother looking for him

Travelling Through Rough Waters

to kill him. The man disguised Himself and did not tell Jacob who He was, Jacob decided to fight for his life, so he grabbed the man. They fought until it was almost daybreak.

In the process of fighting Jacob realized that the man was not an ordinary man. Jesus recognized that Jacob realized that he was fighting with Jesus, and He said to Jacob, "Let me go," and Jacob said, "I will not let you go until you bless me" (Gen. 32:24-26). To be in God's Hall of Fame you have to wrestle with the Lord sometimes. When you are in trouble and you call upon the Lord for help and He does not come, you just don't give up. You must cry out like Jacob: "Lord, I will not let you go until you bless me." The woman with the issue of blood said, If I could only touch the hem of His garment I will be made whole. Jacob got himself into God's Hall of Fame by wrestling with God. Do you think that you could get into God's Hall of Fame by wrestling with Him about your evil propensities and inclinations?

Moses's Qualification to God's Hall of Fame

By faith the parents of Moses went against the king's command to kill all baby boys. They were not afraid to hide their son for the first three months of his life because they believed that he was no ordinary child and that God had a special reason for him to live. Moses showed this same faith all through his youth. He refused to become emotionally attached to Pharaoh or even to be called the son of Pharaoh's daughter. He chose to suffer persecution with God's people rather than to stay at the palace and enjoy the pleasures of sin for a few short years. He regarded

How Does One Get to Be in God's Hall of Fame?

disgrace and scorn for the sake of Christ of more value than all the treasures of Egypt. He looked away from this world and steadily focused on the reward God promised His people. (Heb. 11:23-29, *Clear Word Bible*)

Moses was raised up in wealth; he was the grandson of the king of Egypt, and attended the most prestigious schools of Egypt. One day he tried to intervene by breaking up a fight between two Hebrew men and got in trouble. He ran away from Egypt into the wilderness, and for forty years Moses attended the sheep of Jethro. One day as he was attending the sheep he saw a burning bush, but the bush was not consumed by the fire. Moses was about to go and see this strange phenomenon when a voice came tumbling down the mountainside: "Moses, take off your shoes from off your feet for the place you are standing is holy ground." I completed my education in Egypt, and all seemed to be well with me. Just forty years old and I am ready to do God's work. Where was God when I had to run from Egypt? Why didn't he come to my refuge? But the voice kept ringing, "Moses, take off your shoes from off your feet for the place you are standing is holy ground.

Moses, when God is ready to use you, you are ready. Moses, you do not know when you are ready, but I know when you are ready to be used." All the riches of Egypt would not do for Moses, for he is looking for a city that has a foundation and whose builder and maker is God. Like Moses, for some of us to be in God's Hall of Fame we must be willing to spend forty years in the wilderness without complaining. Moses was forty years old when he was in Egypt; he was next in line for the throne.

Travelling Through Rough Waters

When God chose him to be in His Hall of Fame he was now eighty years old. Sometimes it takes some of us a long time to learn. I also learned from Moses that our timetable is not God's timetable, and God never goes by our timetable, because His name is El-Roi, the God who sees the future, and he knows what is best for us.

Moses thought that he was ready at the age of forty years old. He went to his countrymen to show them the right way, but he was not ready until he was eighty years old, when God told him to take off his shoes from off his feet. You and I might think that we are ready to carry on our everyday life in the world, but we are not ready to take up our citizenship in heaven, so God will send us to the wilderness for five years, ten years, or even forty years until we are ready. Moses was inducted into God's Hall of Fame because he was willing to spend forty years in the wilderness without complaining about it.

Rahab's Qualification to God's Hall of Fame

"Rahab, the Canaanite prostitute in Jericho, believed in the God of Israel and was not killed with those who refused to believe. By faith she welcomed the spies and hid them at the risk of her own life" (Heb. 11:31, *Clear Word Bible*). Rahab, a prostitute? Being a part of God's Hall of Fame? Certainly, a prostitute is not somebody many of us expected to see in God's Hall of Fame. Rahab was standing on the street corner doing her thing. But the spies came along and asked her if she knew where they could hide. These men were from the Israelite army; they came to Jericho to check out the land. They got through the gate unnoticed, but someone told the authorities

How Does One Get to Be in God's Hall of Fame?

that strangers were in town. A manhunt was activated and the men of God had to run for cover.

Rahab was sympathetic to God's business and she helped His servants, by providing a place for them to hide. She asked the men of God, when you come to overthrow this city, will you spare my life? They told her yes, and years later when Joshua marched around Jericho, the wall fell down and the same spies went into the city and got Rahab out before the city was destroyed. I found out that even the ungodly can be a part of God's Hall of Fame. All they've got to do is to repent of their sin and accept Jesus Christ as their personal Savior. Rahab found her way into God's Hall of Fame because she was sympathetic to the affairs of God and stopped the business of prostitution. Do you care anything about God's business? Could it be that your love for God's affairs in your corner of the world provide a way of entering into God's Hall of Fame?

Gideon's Qualification to God's Hall of Fame

"There are many such people of faith, but there isn't time for me to tell you about Gideon, Barak, Samson, Jephthah, David, Samuel and the prophets" (Heb. 11:32). In Judges 6:11-40 we find the story of Gideon. Someone said Gideon reminds us of the power of weakness. Gideon reminds us of the local members in the church who oftentimes don't feel qualified to stand and lead out in the service of the church. They are shy, and timid, and easily offended. If God wants to use them He has to give them proof that He is going to be with them. They

Travelling Through Rough Waters

will not be caught out there by themselves, because they do not trust themselves. They have childlike faith in God and with gentle leading they will do the work of God. Gideon told the Lord, if you plan to use me like you said to lead Israel, I am going lay a piece of wool outside on the ground. If it is your will for me to lead this war, let the dew wet the wool, but the ground around it be dry. God did just what he asked Him to do. Gideon, still timid and shy, said, please do not get upset with me, Lord, but I am going to put another piece of wool out tonight and this time just let the ground around it be wet and the wool be dry. God did what Gideon asked him and the next morning Gideon decided to lead out as Captain.

God told Gideon that he had too many men for war, so 22,000 men left the company of Gideon, leaving him with only about 10,000 men. God told Gideon, "You still have too many men to fight the war," so 9,700 more of the men went home, leaving Gideon with only 300 men. From 32,000 men it came down to 300 men. God told Gideon that the 300 men would suffice. By this time Gideon had grown in faith to the point that he did not care anymore about manpower, because he came to the realization that the battle is for the Lord, and the gate of hell cannot stand up against God. I found out from the story of Gideon that the local church members can also be a part of God's Hall of Fame if they put their trust in God and follow His lead. God will take your little faith and multiply it. You will do things you never thought that you could do. You will mount up like eagles; you will flap your wings and do great things for the church and your fellow men. Gideon used a simple piece of wool and

How Does One Get to Be in God's Hall of Fame?

carved a pathway into God's Hall of Fame. He did not have a lot, but he built on what he had. Somebody said that a little becomes a lot when you placed it in the Master's hand. Gideon's message to all the grasshopper-mentality Christians is: "You, too, can be in God's Hall of Fame."

David's Qualification to God's Hall of Fame

Finally, David was also in God's Hall of Fame. Many people think that he should not be there because he did some of the most despicable things in the Bible. Why was he inducted into God's Hall of Fame? What characteristic did David have that made him a candidate for God's Hall of Fame? Two things: David loved God dearly, and he was kind and tender-hearted to his fellow men. First of all, it was God who said David was a man after His own heart. When a mother or a father says a child has a special place in his heart or her heart, what does this statement mean? Well, it means that the child is obedient, she can count on her child, the child will obey her words and do what she asks him or her to do. The child is understanding and compassionate toward the parent. It does not mean that the child will not make mistakes, but the basic personality is approved by the parent. And don't be mistaken; a mother knows her children.

God said I know David and I approve of his basic personality toward me and his fellow men. It does not mean that David did not have some serious problems, but God said I know him and he is a man of my own heart. Let us look quickly at two references into David's true nature. David took Uria's wife then devised a plan and killed

Travelling Through Rough Waters

Uria. The Lord confronted him and told him that He was going to punish him severely. David said to the Lord, "I am sorry, please forgive me of my sin." And he waited for his punishment. He did not complain, and he did not make excuses. When God started the punishment and the heavy hand of God was coming down on David, he cried out, "God have mercy on me." He had not said a word, he did not complain, he just asked God to have mercy. How many times when you are about to chastise your child, and because of their humbleness and respect for you, your heart just could not allow you to continue? God loves a childlike heart.

Just one more look at his attitude toward people. David was on his way to help fight with the Philistines, but some of the Philistine leaders did not trust him, so they told him to go back home (1 Sam. 29:3-6). When David got back home, some guerrillas invaded the city and took their possessions and families. David decided to go after them, and told the fighting men to come with him. More than half of them did not go because they were mad with him. Those who were willing went and God gave David the victory and he was able to bring back all their goods along with the wives and children. When they got back home, those men who went to battle decided to take everything, including the wives and children who belonged to those men who did not go with them. David came and said, it does not matter that they did not go with us, let every body have equal share and give back to every man their wives and children. God smiled when David enforced the rule (1 Sam. 30:1-15).

That is how David deals with his fellow man. He is kind and loving just like his heavenly Father. He does not hold

How Does One Get to Be in God's Hall of Fame?

grudges. Saul had been chasing him for almost twenty years to kill him. He found Saul sleeping in a cave and he went over and cut off a piece of his overcoat just to let him know that he could have killed him if he wanted to; but then he felt guilty because he had cut the king's garment. When David heard that Saul was dead, this was his reaction: "When David heard this, he tore his clothes in grief and broke down and wept and so did all his men. All day they mourned for Saul and his sons and for all the Israelites who had been killed in battle. They wept and did not eat because Israel had been defeated" (2 Sam. 1:11-12).

David's ticket to God's Hall of Fame is his willingness to surrender to God's leading in is life and being kind and loving to his fellow men. How about you? Do you resist God's leading and His command? Are you kind to people and forgive them when they do wrong to you? Please be advised that you could be inducted into God's Hall of Fame by just being nice to people and obeying God's word.

The people who are in the Hall of Fame are famous. Their names are on billboards, they are on TV, and many of them are on Cornflakes boxes; but one day God's Hall of Famers will walk the street of goal in Heaven, we shall follow the Lamb wherever He goes. We will live with Jesus in the earth made new. Jesus will leave heaven one day and He will come to earth and gather all His people, and we will live forever with Jesus. In our world today, only a few people get inducted into the Hall of Fame, but all of God's children will be in God's Hall of Fame. Let us not resist His leading, because He is leading us to His Hall of Fame.

Chapter 22

Homosexuals - and the Bible

I almost did not write this chapter of the book. I taught about the subject, but because of the uneasiness of the subject in our communities across the country I decided to leave the subject alone. After the book was edited and was ready to be sent to the Interior Designer, I woke up one morning at 5 o'clock with an overpowering urge to write this chapter that I had left out of the book. I got up immediately and started writing. I felt that I had left out

Homosexuals - and the Bible

an important subject out of the book, and I was ready to start writing. I have spoken to many people about the practices of homosexuals, and the teachings of the bible, and as the faces of these people are different, so are their ideas about the subject. I thought to myself that the only place I am going to get a straight answer from is the Bible, so I turned to the word of God to see how God feels about this matter.

God's plan is always the best plan, because He knows about yesterday, He knows about today, and He knows about tomorrow, so it is always best to follow God's plan. God decided to create the human family on planet earth, and He created a man and a woman. The man was created first, and he was lonely and needed a companion. God also wanted to replenish the earth, so He made for the man a woman. And the Lord God said, "It is not good that man should be alone; I will make him a helper comparable to him." (Genesis 2:18).

Genesis 2:18 makes it very clear that if a man is lonely and needs a companion he needs to get a woman, and if a woman is lonely and needs a companion she needs to get a man. When man was lonely and needed a companion God gave him a woman. The homosexuals may say, "I do not feel for a person of the same sex. My feelings are legitimate, I did not made myself feel this way, therefore, my feelings should be taken into consideration.

Isaiah 1: 5-6 responds to the homosexuals' legitimate feelings, by telling us that we must be careful of our feelings because our head is sick and there is no soundness in it. "...The whole head is sick and the whole heart faint. 1:6 from the sole of the foot even unto the head, there is

Travelling Through Rough Waters

no soundness in it, but wounds, and bruises and puttying sores." (Isaiah 1:5-6).

We do not know at what time after the creation of mankind that homosexual practices started, but I suppose it was going on behind the scenes, because in Leviticus 18:22 God told the Christian community in bible days that a Man should not lie with another man as with a women, it is an abomination. (Leviticus 18:22). The word abomination is a very strong and serious word to be used by God. The word is translated from the Hebrew word, "Toebah" indicating a violation of divinely established customs and practices, such as sexual aberration. (Aberration refers to a deviation from the proper or expected course, or a departure from the normal.), so in other words, God told His children not to lie in bed with a person of the same sex, because such a practice is a deviation from the divinely established principles. The practice is abnormal and God frowns upon such practices.

God equates the practice of homosexuality with the practice of idolatry. In Deuteronomy 12:31 God used the same word (abomination) to described the practice of idolatry among the heathen. He said, "You shall not do so to The Lord your God. For every abominable thing which The Lord hates they have done for their gods. For even their sons and their daughters they have burned in the fire of their gods." (Deut. 12:31). The Lord told His people that the ungodly people worship idols and offered their children in the fire to their gods, but the children of God should not do such things. "You shall not behave this way toward The Lord your God." (Deut. 12:4).

Homosexuals - and the Bible

All through the scripture you will notice God's disapproval of homosexual activity. Let us look at a few of these quotations:

Lev. 18:22-25
"Do not have sex with another male. That is detestable. You are not to have sex with an animal, nor is a woman to present herself to an animal for sex. That is a perversion. You are not to defile yourself in any of these ways, for that is how the people in the land where I am taking you are defiling themselves. That is why I am driving them out from this fruitful land and making room for you. Their perverted natures have defiled the whole land. Therefore I have withheld my blessings and the land is vomiting them out." (Lev. 18:22-25).

Matthew 19:3-4
The Pharisees were tempting Christ and asking Him question about marriage, and Jesus alluded to the creation story. He said to them, "Have you not read that He which made them at the beginning made them male and female?" (Matthew 19:3-4). Based on the above statement, Christ only condones sexual relationship between a man and a woman.

Romans 1:18-32
"So God couldn't do for them what He would like to have done. He let them do what they wanted to do, no matter how revolting it was to Him. They were so lustful and filthy that they ravished each other's bodies and behaved more like animals than humans. God, being the

Travelling Through Rough Waters

kind of God that He is, didn't just step in and take away their freedom of choice. So they abused their freedom and did their own thing. Even their women departed from the Creator's pattern for them and engaged in all kinds of unnatural acts with other women. Their men were no different. They went against the Creator's design for them and lusted after other men. Men were having sex with men, then reaping in themselves the results of their willful disregard of God's law. Because they didn't want to recognize God as their Creator and keep Him in mind, their thinking became twisted, their actions gross, and they ended up doing all sorts of things people should never do. Their lives became filled with every kind of wrongdoing, such as sexual abuse, perverseness, jealousy, maliciousness, greed, fighting, lying, hatred and murder." (Romans 1:18-32). This is the first time the bible specifically refers to women involved in lesbianism. The bible made it very plain that these women departed from the Creator's pattern for them and engaged in all kinds of unnatural acts with other women.

1 Corinthians. 6:9-11

"Don't you know that evildoers will not inherit the kingdom? Don't be fooled. Those who are immoral, who worship idols, commit adultery, practice homosexuality, (effeminate) abuse themselves or others sexually, who steal, lie, cheat, get drunk, slander and defraud others—none of these will have a part in God's kingdom." (1 Corinthians 6:9-11). So, based on 1 Corinthians 6:9-11, homosexuals are among a group of people who will not be save in God's kingdom if they continue to practice these activities.

Gelation 5:19-22
"The actions of our sinful nature are obvious: sexual immorality, impure thoughts, filthy language and recklessness, just to mention a few. But they don't end there. They also include idolatry, witchcraft, hatred, discord, and jealousy, fits of rage, selfish ambition, strife, hostility, heresies, envy, drunkenness and sexual perversions. There are other evils committed which I'm not going to mention because you already know what they are. I'm warning you again "those who do these things cannot be taken into God's kingdom." (Galatian 5:19-22).

Homosexual insisted on having a permanent place in society.
During the bible days, the practice of homosexuality, reached to its highest level during the Sodom and Gomorrah saga. The story started in Genesis chapter 18. Abraham was sitting at the door of his house, under the Oaks tree during the heat of the day. He looked up and saw three men standing at his gate. He got up and went to meet them. He greeted them respectfully and invited them to his house. Abraham was very hospitable to the men. He gave them water to wash their feet. (It was the custom in those days to wash the feet of strangers when they come to your house.) He fed them and asked them to rest before they continued their journey. The men agreed and Abraham called a few of his servants and had them quickly butcher a young calf and prepared it

Travelling Through Rough Waters

for the men. While the men were eating, Abraham stood by them and watched them. One of the man said to Abraham, "Where is Sarah your wife?" Abraham said, "She is here in the tent" and the Man who was The Lord said to Abraham, "Sarah your wife will have a son." Sarah was in the tent listening to the conversation with the men and her husband, and when the man told Abraham that she would have a son she laughed, because she had past the age of childbearing.

The Man who was God, saw when Sarah laughed and He asked Abraham, "Why did Sarah laugh?" Sarah denied that she laughed, because she was afraid, but the Lord said to her, "You did laugh." The men got up and turned toward Sodom, and Abraham went with them through the gate. One of the Man who was The Lord said, "Shall I hide from Abraham (My friend and my servant) what am I going to do?" The Lord said to Abraham, "The sins of Sodom and Gomorrah is great and their sin is exceedingly grievous. I will go down now and see whether they have done altogether as is the cry of it which has come to Me, and if not, I will know."

While The Lord was talking to Abraham, the other two men who were angels left and went to Sodom. Please note here that St. John 1:18 made it very clear that God the Father has never seen in bodily form, so the person who was among these two angels would be the second person of the Godhead which is Jesus. Genesis chapter 18 picks up the story with these two angels entering the city of Sodom. It was in the evening and two angels came to the gate of Sodom. Lot was sitting at the gate, and as soon as he saw these two men, he got up and went to meet them. He respectfully greeted them and said to them, "My lords, turn aside, I beg of you, into your servant's house and spend the night and bathe your feet, then you can arise early and go on your way."

The two men did not readily accept Lot's offer. They told Lot that they would spend the night in the city's square, but Lot entreated and urged them until they agreed and entered Lot's house. Lot made them dinner and they did eat and drink, but before they laid down, the men of the city of Sodom, both young and old, from every quarters of the city surrounded the house, and they called to Lot and said, "Where are the men who came to your house tonight? Bring them out to us, that we may know them (Meaning to have sex with them). Lot went outside to the men and shut the door behind him. Lot said to the men, "I beg you, my brothers, do not behave so wickedly. Look! I have two daughters who are virgins, let me bring them out to you and you can do as you please with them, but please do not do anything to these men for they have come under the protection of my roof."

But the men said to Lot, "Stand back! (And they spoke to each other) These fellow came to live here temporarily, and now he presumes to be our judge?! Now we will deal worse with him than with them." So they rushed and pressed violently against Lot, and they came close to breaking the door down. Then one of the visiting men, (Who was an angel) reached out and pulled Lot into the house and shut the door. And they struck the men, both young and old, who were at the door with blindness, so they were not able to find the door. The two men asked

Travelling Through Rough Waters

Lot, "Have you any others here, sons-in-law, sons, or daughters? Whomever you have in this city bring them out of this place. For we will spoil and destroy Sodom, for the outcry and shriek against its people has grown great before The Lord, and He has sent us to destroy it." (The word, "shriek" indicates a loud, or a cry that has a high pitched. This word is used many times in the text. This constant reoccurring indicates that the situation in Sodom and Gomorrah caught God's attention. It was a big concern in heaven, and God had to do something about it.)

Lot went out and told his sons-in-law who were to married his daughters to get out of the city because The Lord was going to destroy the city, but they thought that he was joking. At day break, the angels urged Lot to hurry. They said, "Arise, take your wife and two daughters who are here with you and be gone, lest you too be consumed and swept away in the iniquity and punishment of the city." But Lot still lingered, and the angels seized him and his wife and his two daughters by the hand, because The Lord was merciful to him, and they brought him forth and set him outside of the city and left him there. The angels told Lot and his family to escape for their lives and they should not look back. Then The Lord rained on Sodom and on Gomorrah brimstone and fire from The Lord out of heaven.

Genesis 19:25 tells us that Sodom and Gomorrah were not the only cities that got burned up. All the other cities that were within the vicinity were burned up as well, which means that all the cities within the area were involved in the practice of homosexuality. I told you earlier that the third person that was left speaking to Abraham was the second Person of the Godhead. There is something important in this text that I would like you to pay close attention to. I do not want you to miss it. Genesis 19:24 tells us that The Lord rained on Sodom and Gomorrah brimstone and fire from The Lord out of heaven.

Did you get the point? The first Person of the Godhead (Who is God the Father) is in heaven and the second Person of the Godhead (Who is Jesus Christ) is on the earth, and He ignited the fire on Sodom and Gomorrah through the authority of God, Who is the first Person of the Godhead and who is in heaven? The Greeks or the original language said it very clearly, because they use different endings for the name of God, which is describing for us who is doing the acting as it relates to the Godhead. The Godhead designed their plan for the universe and the second person of the Godhead (Jesus) carries out the plan. Jesus is the visible One who creates everything in heaven and in this world. (Colossians 1:16, John 1:1-3). He dies for the people of this world, and He helps the people of this world in the plan of redemption. The original language help us to differentiate which Person of the Godhead was in Sodom and Gomorrah, and who was carrying out the actions in Sodom. For example, In the Greek or the original language, "*Qeouos*" is the word for God, and "*Qeouon*" indicates which Person of the Godhead who is carrying out the action. In Genesis 19:24 the original language would be read differently from the way the King James Version reads, it reads, "*Qeouon* rained down fire and brimstone on

Travelling Through Rough Waters

Sodom and Gomorrah from *Qeouos* in heaven." By this we understand that it is Jesus, the second Person of the Godhead who igniting the fire on Sodom and Gomorrah through the authority of God the Father, the first Person of the Godhead who was in heaven. So the situation with the homosexuals are very serious. In the past, the second Person of the Godhead had to leave heaven and come to planet earth to deal with this very situation, and the way things are looking right now, He might have to come back to deal with the same situation again.

Do homosexuals have a right to practice homosexuality, while claiming rights among Christian believers?

First of all, let us remind ourselves what the word "Christian" means. The word Christian means followers of Jesus. This concept indicates that people who claim to be Christians must do what God tells them to do. If a person decides to live his or her life the way he wants to live, not taking into consideration God's rules and principles of the Christian's faith, this individual cannot claim ranks among those people who have decided to restrain from the desires of the flesh and follow God's word. The scripture shows over and over that God dislikes the practice of homosexuality. Please notice that I say, "The practice" not the person. God loves all the people in the world, including the people who practice homosexual acts, but He hates their practice. Someone may say, "And how do you know God's mind, Mr. God's spokesman?" Well, previously I highlighted many quotations from the bible that provide a synopsis view of God will toward

Homosexuals - and the Bible

the practice of homosexuals' acts.

In Genesis 19:24 we see the second Person of the Godhead leaving heaven and came to earth to deal with people who practice homosexuals acts. Genesis 19:24 tells us that God's action was very severe against these people. He burned them up in Sodom and Gomorrah. A homosexual has an individual right to live his or her life has he or she sees fit, but they do not have a right to impose their practice upon the Christian church, because Jesus is the leader of the Christian church and He condemns their practice. The following texts verified this said point. (1 Corinthians. 6:9-11, Lev.18:22-25, Romans 1:18-32)

Ellen G. White commented on the story of Sodom and Gomorrah and this is what she said, "The sun was risen upon the earth when Lot entered into Zoar." The bright rays of the morning seemed to speak only prosperity and peace to the cities of the plain. The stir of active life began in the streets; men were going their various ways, intent on the business or the pleasures of the day. The sons-in-law of Lot were making merry at the fears and warnings of the weak-minded old man. Suddenly and unexpectedly as would be a thunder peal from an unclouded sky, the tempest broke. The Lord rained brimstone and fire out of heaven upon the cities and the fruitful plain; its palaces and temples, costly dwellings, gardens and vineyards, and the gay, pleasure-seeking throngs that only the night before had insulted the messengers of heaven—all were consumed.

The smoke of the conflagration went up like the smoke of a great furnace. And the fair veil of Sodom became a desolation, a place never to be built up or

Travelling Through Rough Waters

inhabited—a witness to all generations of the certainty of God's judgments upon transgression. The flames that consumed the cities of the plain shed their warning light down even to our time. We are taught the fearful and solemn lesson that while God's mercy bears long with the transgressor, there is a limit beyond which men may not go on in sin. When that limit is reached, then the offers of mercy are withdrawn, and the ministration of judgment begins. There can be no compromise between God and the world, you cannot serve God and mammon." (Ellen G. White, Patriarchs and Prophets, Ch. 13. "Destruction of Sodom".)

Conclusion

Base on the word of God, homosexuals acts are sins just like any other sin. (I should point out, however, that God has a strong dislike for homosexual acts. He told Abraham that the practice was great and their sin was exceedingly grievous. (Gen. 18:20) If homosexuals repent and forsake their sin they can be saved in God's kingdom. Based on the word of God, homosexual and lesbians cannot be save in God's kingdom while practicing the act of homosexuality. Homosexuals may say, "I was born with feeling of wanting people from the same sex." Well, all of us were born with feelings that we have to resist if we want to be saved in God's kingdom. There are people who were born in this world with desires to steal, desires to kill, desires to lie, desires to be covetous, and the list goes on, but we all must resist sinful feelings if we want to be saved in God's kingdom. God condemns the practice of homosexuality the same way

Homosexuals - and the Bible

He condemns stealing, murder and lying.

Anyone who continue to steal, murder and lie, cannot be saved in God's kingdom. If a homosexual wants to claim ranks among the Christian community, he or she should ask God to help him or her to give up homosexual practices, because the bible said people who do these things could have some problems in getting into the kingdom of God. "Don't you know that evildoers will not inherit the kingdom? Don't be fooled. Those who are immoral, who worship idols, commit adultery, practice homosexuality, (effeminate) abuse themselves or others sexually, who steal, lie, cheat, get drunk, slander and defraud others—none of these will have a part in God's kingdom." (1 Corinthians 6:9-11).

www.ingramcontent.com/pod-product-compliance
Lightning Source LLC
Chambersburg PA
CBHW050854160426
43194CB00011B/2151